Intrepid Americans:
Bold Koreans

Front piece 1: Chosôn Dynasty Korea Nineteenth Century Map

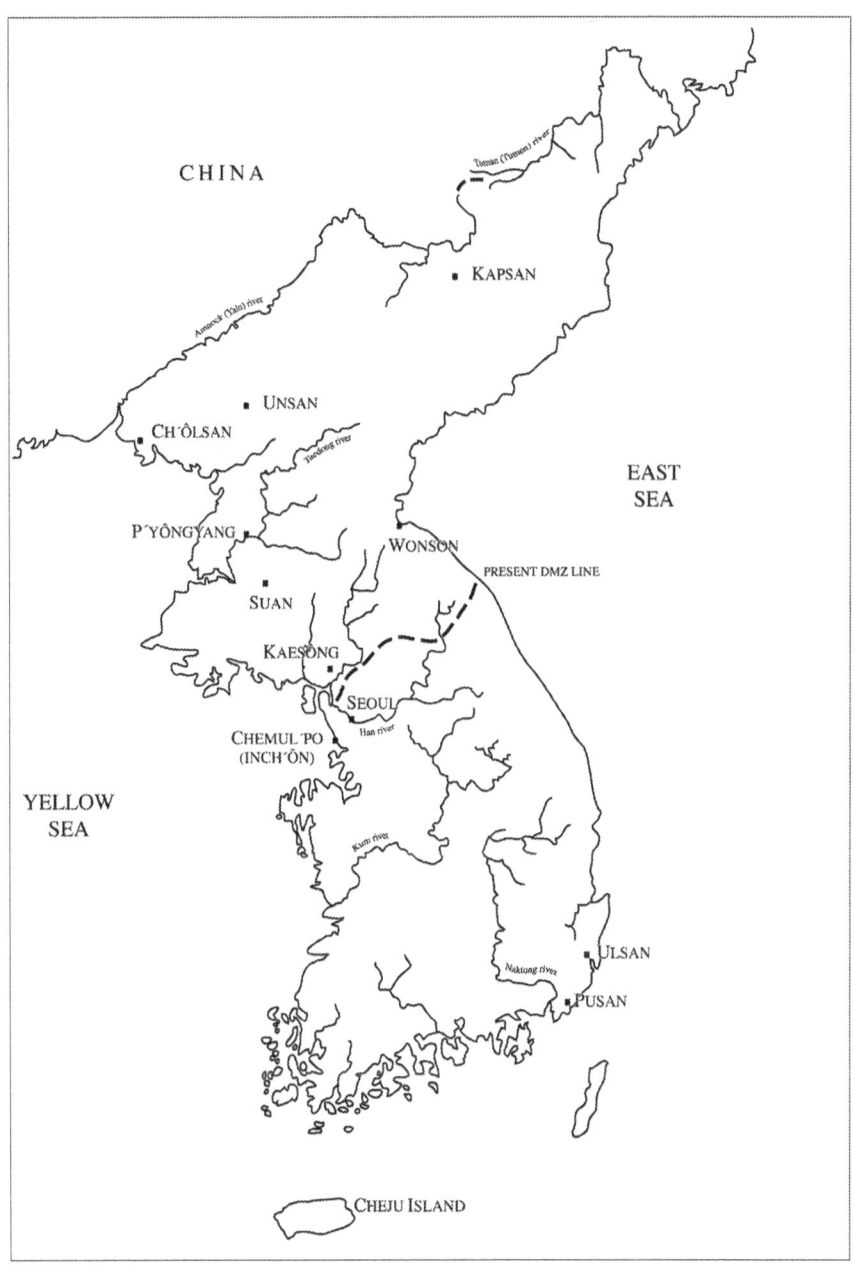

CHINA

Tuman (Tumen) river

KAPSAN

Amnock (Yalu) river

UNSAN

CH'ÔLSAN

Taedong river

EAST
SEA

P'YÔNGYANG

WONSON

PRESENT DMZ LINE

SUAN

KAESONG

SEOUL

CHEMUL'PO
(INCH'ÔN)

Han river

YELLOW
SEA

Kum river

ULSAN

Naktong river

PUSAN

CHEJU ISLAND

Front piece 2: Western Map of Korea, Early Modern Era, with locations discussed in this text.

Intrepid Americans: Bold Koreans—Early Korean Trade, Concessions, And Entrepreneurship

Donald G. Southerton

iUniverse, Inc.
New York Lincoln Shanghai

Intrepid Americans: Bold Koreans—Early Korean Trade, Concessions, And Entrepreneurship

iUniverse books may be ordered through booksellers or by contacting:

iUniverse
2021 Pine Lake Road, Suite 100
Lincoln, NE 68512
www.iuniverse.com
1-800-Authors (1-800-288-4677)

ISBN-13: 978-0-595-37068-9 (pbk)
ISBN-13: 978-0-595-81470-1 (ebk)
ISBN-10: 0-595-37068-3 (pbk)
ISBN-10: 0-595-81470-0 (ebk)

Printed in the United States of America

To those intrepid nineteenth century Anglos who voyaged to Korea in search of opportunity and profit. And, to those equally bold Koreans who embraced change, challenged risk, and sought trade and commerce.

Their stories continue to inspire me...

Contents

Illustrations

Figures

Maps

Charts

Acknowledgements

Crafting an accurate account of a nation's past is not without its challenges. Crafting an account of Korea in the late nineteenth century brings with it additional demands including language barriers and nearly a century of histories often woven with agendas that include Japanese Colonialism, Korean nationalism, and even North Korean revisionism.

A number of people graciously aided in the research and writing of this book. I feel it is only fitting for a work that highlights the interactions of Anglos and Koreans that many Americans and Koreans assisted in this project.

First, throughout the writing of the book my longtime language partner and skilled Korean linguist Yongjoon Cho was highly supportive, encouraging, and helpful. While I attended classes at the University of Southern California, Professor Kyung Moon Hwang and In Soo Cho provided insights into Korean history and culture. At UCLA, I was fortunate to have benefited from Luce Foundation Visiting Scholar Chai-Sik Chung of Boston and Yonsei Universities. Dr. Chung's frank classroom lectures, complimented several one-on-one conversations whereby I gained a deeper understanding of early Protestantism in Korea. Professor Chung also graciously read a portion of the manuscript in its early stages. Equally supportive of this work, especially with regard to Henry Collbran and Harry Bostwick's efforts in Korea, was Professor Ki-Seok Kim of Seoul National University. In addition, Dr. Kim helped me gain access to digital archives at Seoul National University—a project he supported and instituted.

As a resource for better understanding late nineteenth century mining and Colorado history during Henry Collbran's years in Denver, Professor James (Jay) E. Fell, Jr. has proved a wealth of knowledge. Moreover his interest in my academic work over the years is appreciated.

I would also like to thank my instructors, Professors Leonid Petrov, Hilary Finchum-Sung, and Jacqueline Pak, who read and corrected portions of the manuscript while I was affiliated with the Intercultural Institute of California.

Their expert suggestions, critiques, and comments in the manuscript's early stages added substantially to the work's scholarship.

More recently, I have benefited from an association with the University of California, San Diego School of International Relations and Pacific Studies. Through an affiliation with the school's Korea Pacific Program and Professor Stephan Haggard, my political and economic views of Korea have deepened and widened.

While researching this project I benefited from the following institutions and their helpful staffs: the University of Southern California's Von Kleinsmid, Doheny Memorial, and Korean Heritage Libraries; the University of California, Los Angeles' Young Research and East Asian Libraries; the University of California, San Diego's Geisel and International Relations and Pacific Studies Research Libraries; the University of Colorado, Denver's Auraria Library; the University of Colorado, Boulder's Norlin Library; Denver Public Library; the Colorado Historical Society's Hart Library, and the San Francisco Cable Car Museum.

Several acknowledgments remain, each deserve special mention. First, I would like to thank my language partners Young Shin Park, Seok Kyu Choi, and Chul Ho Kim. Their assistance in discussions and researching topics in Korean source archives is appreciated.

Next, I would like to thank Mark S. Foster, Professor Emeritus, University of Colorado, Denver. Without his encouragement to pursue an interest in writing, this book would have remained but a collection of thoughts.

In addition, while at an impasse in the structuring of this work, I benefited greatly from the expert advice of Vera Caccioppoli of the Hi-Way-Haven writing center.

Finally, Anna Cash-Mitchell has truly been a partner in this work from first draft to final copy. Outside her copious reading of the manuscript and numerous editorial suggestions, Anna's creative and technical skills ensured that the rich illustrations added an amazing dimension to the book. Her assistance throughout the project warrants a very special thanks.

Foreword

Research and the initial writings for this book started in 2002, when I was attending graduate school at the University of Colorado, Denver. I became intrigued in the accounts of Anglo travelers to Korea during the late nineteenth century. These accounts described firsthand impressions of the land and its people. Two thoughts surfaced, first how rapidly change occurred on the East Asian peninsula with the introduction of westernization and modernization. And secondly, how well century-old photographs depict daily life in Korea, especially in documenting the arrival of western technology such as trolleys and electric lighting.

As my readings and research unfolded, I came to see that American influence heralded much of the change in Korea, particularly with the introduction of western technology connected to business ventures. Moreover, it becomes apparent that unlike the other outsiders who offered much needed military, governmental, and bureaucratic expertise. American concessionaires and interestingly, American Protestant missionaries, fostered another aspect of the West—business, capitalism, and entrepreneurship—a theme I have woven throughout this work.

In this work, the reader will see a number of Korean terms. These terms are romanized according to the McCune-Reischauer method. The romanized Korean terms used in the book have also been listed in the glossary. Historic names such as Syngman Rhee are written in manner familiar to most westerners; however, all other Korean names use a traditional surname first format. For example, Chung Hee Park will be shown as Park Chung Hee.

Chapter One
Introduction

This book is a detailed study of noteworthy interactions and significant events in the early development of U.S.-Korean trade, commerce, and business relations. Relevant to the study of contemporary South Korea, the reader will gain an understanding into how radically Korea's economy transformed over the last century from a developed agrarian market to modern capitalistic, industrialized society. In fact, today capitalism, accumulation of individual wealth, and conspicuous consumption can be seen as great markers of modern Korean society.[1] Perhaps, one of the most fascinating dimensions of this book is the role intrepid Americans played in introducing modernization, heralding capitalism, kindling entrepreurialism, and fostering business development on East Asian peninsular Korea.[2]

Defining Entrepreneurialism

In the course of crafting this work, a subject that continued to re-surface was Korean entrepreneurship. First, economists accept no single definition of entrepreneurship or one that fits all economies and eras. For example, Alfred Marshall in his 1890 classic *Principles of Economics* noted that entrepreneurs were the driving force behind industry, act with limited information, and that entrepreneurship was a rare skill. In contrast, noted economist Harvey Leibenstein argues that the dominant characteristic of entrepreneurs is their ability to perceive gaps in markets. They then develop new goods, services, or processes to fit those needs. Moreover, Leibenstein points out that entrepreneurs have the ability to innovatively combine various inputs to satisfy the market. In turn, esteemed management guru Peter Drucker in *Innovation and Entrepreneurship: Practice and Principles* found that in some cases, entrepreneurs may not produce a new product but use creative innovation to apply knowledge and technology developed elseware to their local market niche.

Nevertheless, by combining respective theories I have arrived at a generalized set of qualities that apply well to both the intrepid Anglos and bold Koreans discussed in this book. They include risk takers, organizers, coordinators, gap-fillers, and innovators.[3]

Recent Change

Fig. 1.1 1960s Korean-made Goldstar (now LG Electronics) Black and White Television.

Fig. 1.2 Early Korean-made export automobile: 1986 Hyundai Pony (marketed in the U.S. as the Excel)

Recent history records that in the wake of World War II and the subsequent Korean War of the early 1950s, the United States and South Korea developed a mutually beneficial tie.[4] A dimension of this was rooted in the United States' global policy for containment of communism. This meant that nations such as South Korea received massive economic assistance while America also served as a market for inexpensively produced Korean goods. Although their political relationship has been at times hot and cold, trade grew dramatically during the last quarter of the twentieth century as South Korean export-driven manufacturing produced billions of dollars in low-cost electronics, textiles, and automobiles for the American consumer market. More impressive are the tremendous economic inroads of the new millennium, where South Korea's top conglomerates command impressive global market shares in the construction, shipbuilding, automotive, appliance, chemical, and electronics sectors.

Fig. 1.3 Just over a century ago Korea opened to the West, today it is a world leader in a number of market sectors including consumer electronics, telecommunications, and car manufacturing. (Samsung digital camcorder, Hyundai Sonata, LG Plasma HD Screen, Kia Sportage, LG cell phone and Samsung cell phone)

Stepping Back

Interestingly, economic ties between Korea and the United States began over a century ago, when entrepreneurial American merchants and businessmen sought new global markets and Korea was perceived as an untouched and yet to be exploited "Hermit Kingdom."[5] Accordingly, the early chapters of this text will provide background and framework to better understand the barriers to western-style trade and commerce. For example, Chapter Two of this book probes the nineteenth century socio-political dynamics of Neo-Confucian Korea's isolationist policy. One will also learn how influential elites within Korea saw western religion, mannerism, and thought as polluting and degrading influences—not to mention that some in Korea saw little need for westernization. This was not without merit since Korea for centuries had a remarkably stable society and sound advanced agrarian economy. This mindset will in Chapter Two be contrasted to the West's desire to expand mercantile interests into new markets—whether they were wanted or not.

Next, Chapter Three provides a fascinating narrative and in-depth account into the first attempt by American traders to openly venture into Korea's inland waterways—the ill-fated voyage of the *General Sherman*.[6] This chapter seeks to answer long asked questions that the ship and its voyage into Korean waters have provoked. For the West, the subsequent attack on the *Sherman* and its crew by inhabitants of the P'yŏngyang area seemed unwarranted and even barbaric. To the Koreans, their hostile actions would seem quite justified.

Chapter Four, in-turn, examines the murky diplomatic waters surrounding the *Sherman* and her crew's fate. The reader will come to understand the difficulties officials encountered in East Asia where American diplomats were naively unfamiliar with the region's norms, policies, and customs. Chapter Five, after surveying changes that led to the softening of Korean isolationist policy and opening to western trade, finds the United States government entering into a long in coming formal trade relationship with Korea. This concurrently heralded progressive reforms on the East Asian peninsula that unfolded as concessions, capitalism, and Korean entrepreurialism, the topic of chapters Six and Seven. Of note, readers of this book will discover in Chapter Six first hand accounts of life in Korea, especially in its capital city of Seoul. The chapter then highlights the entrepreneurial efforts of Henry Collbran, who with partner Harry Bostwick succeeded in obtaining lucrative concessions that included the Seoul electric trolley line, lighting system, waterworks, a movie theater, and prized mining rights for gold and copper in what is today North Korea.

Chapter Seven shifts from narrative to an analysis, commentary, and discussion of early Korean capitalism that emerged in the late nineteenth century. Chapter Seven first looks at the impact of western enterprises like those of American concessionaire Henry Collbran on fostered early Korean entrepreneurship. This chapter also covers the impact of the Christian Protestant mission's capitalist gospel and its leadership including Horace Grant Underwood, whose affluent family owned the Underwood Typewriter Company. The chapter then explores the controversial origin of Korean capitalism. With relevancy today, Chapter Seven links the traits of early Korean entrepreneurship to characteristics widely recognized and attributed in contemporary society to the success of modern Korean big business.

Finally, this work's concluding chapter seeks to offer lessons learned from early U.S.-Korean trade and commerce—including the revisionist manipulation of the *Sherman* saga for twenty first century North Korean anti-American, anti-imperialist rhetoric. This gains considerable importance as North Korea's foreign and domestic policies have, at the time of this writing, brought uncertainty and instability in the region.

To conclude (or actually begin), this book will provide amazing insights into the birth of modern South Korean entrepreneurialism and commerce. These glimpses presented through photographs, illustrations, narratives, and commentary will give the reader a better appreciation into the recent progress in South Korea, and perhaps, some meaning and dimension to the often over-looked role played by American businessmen on the peninsula. In fact, I see Americans heralding capitalism and entrepreneurship—characteristics, which reemerged in South Korea during the last quarter of the twentieth century and has spurred its phenomenal economic and business development.

Chapter Two
Unwelcome, Unwanted

Confucianism, in stark contrast to the West, placed tight regulations on unbridled commerce and gave scant respect to businessmen.
— *Stewart Lone and Gavin McCormick,* Korea Since 1850

Fig. 2.1 Seoul's Namdaemun (Great South Gate) in a mid nineteenth century depiction of the 600-Year-old mecca for Korean trade and commerce

During the early-to-middle 1800s, western intrusion into Korea was "unwelcome and unwanted."[1] This chapter probes the nineteenth century socio-political dynamics of Neo-Confucian Korea's isolationist policy. This will be contrasted to the West's fervent desire to expand mercantile interests into new untapped markets. Of significance, some Koreans, unlike most westerners, did not see the Korean economy or nation-state as undeveloped or backwards. Moreover, Korea's rulers and members of the aristocratic class of scholar-officials, the *yangban*, had carefully watched the effects of western penetration into China and Japan. Korea's conservative leadership was appalled by their Asian neighbors' violation of the centuries old Confucian norms and attempts at modernization. *Yangban* elitists feared open borders would pollute Korea—a morally superior, self-sufficient, Neo-Confucian state.[2] Moreover, to forsake Confucian traditions and yield to western culture was seen by conservative bureaucrat-officials as the "worst of all heterodoxies" and would ruin Korea.[3]

Stable and Self-Sufficient

For centuries many Koreans perceived their state and domestic agrarian-based economy as stable and self-sufficient institutions. Within Korean society, a rigid Neo-Confucian social stratification existed. Specifically, this meant government leadership and administration was in the hands of the monarchy and the ruling elite, a landed gentry called *yangban,* whose sole occupation was the holding of public office.[4] Adding to the situation was a mindset among the governing elites that agriculture, manufacturing, and commerce were the descending societal roles of farmers, artisans, and merchants. (see Chart 2.1) From the *yangban's* perspective of the later, business and commerce was best delegated to those of lower status and that a *yangban's* focus should be on moral cultivation and the fine arts. So taboo were commercial activities that even poor *yangban* with little income from landholding or public office did not enter into business.[5]

Fig. 2.2 *Threshing Rice*, a genre painting by eighteenth century artist Kim Hong Do. The painting illustrates the four steps in rice threshing, all under the watchful eye of a *yangban* elite.

Fig. 2.3 *Carpenters.* This painting by Kim Hong Do depicts the tasks involved in the construction of a building. Similar to the previous illustration, there is a contrast in the activities of the workers and the overseer (shown standing with a staff). The class distinction between the workers and the overseer is apparent both by the division of labor and through apparel. The Korean workers are depicted shirtless with open tunics, and with rolled-up pant legs—signs of their low-class status. In contrast, the overseer wears a hat and has a long tunic that hangs over his pants, which signify upper-class rank.

Fig. 2.4 *Scholar and Lute.* This third genre painting by Kim Hong Do contrasts with the previous two genre paintings in its more positive portrayal of the *yangban* elite. This illustration portrays the scholar refining and cultivating skills in the arts—literature, poetry, flower painting, calligraphy, and music.

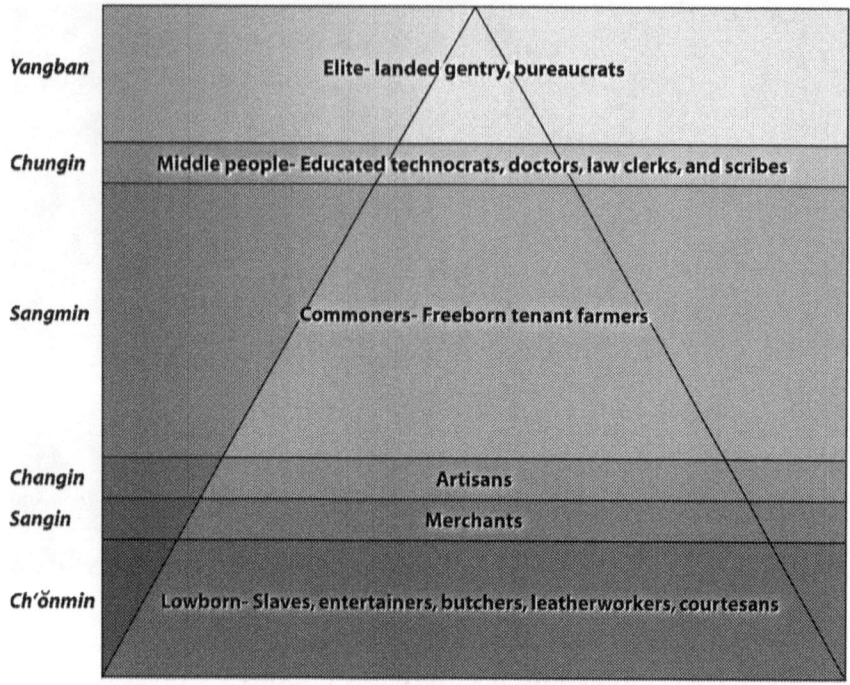

Yangban — Elite- landed gentry, bureaucrats

Chungin — Middle people- Educated technocrats, doctors, law clerks, and scribes

Sangmin — Commoners- Freeborn tenant farmers

Changin — Artisans

Sangin — Merchants

Ch'ŏnmin — Lowborn- Slaves, entertainers, butchers, leatherworkers, courtesans

Chart 2.1 Korean Social Stratification

An Agrarian Economy

Fig. 2.5 Rice farming. During the Chosôn Dynasty Korea's agrarian economy centered on rice production—produced on land

owned by the *yangban* and farmed by the tenant farmers.

By the Early Modern Era, the Korean economy, which had for centuries rested firmly on a mature and advanced agrarian market system, was undergoing change. Since the 1700s, technological advancements meant increased agricultural production with, for example, water for irrigation supplied by over 6,000 reservoirs and double cropping of rice and winter barley.[6] Increased yields and surplus meant some farmer-tenants gradually accumulated wealth, bought land, and even rivaled the *yangban* in landholdings. More profound were the changes to the foreign and domestic trade. Once a state monopoly with the court as the nation's largest consumer of manufactured goods, by the 1700s, successful *kaekchu* (commission agents) and *yôgak* (brokers) challenged the state accredited merchants of the courts.[7] These new entrepreneurs and gap filers acted as middlemen for producers of commercial cash crops such as tobacco, cotton, and ginseng, which the merchants in turn exported at a profit to China and Japan. These bold merchants also developed a brisk inland and coastal trade that included an elaborate system of wholesaling, warehousing, transportation, and even banking. Across Korea, in thousands of towns and villages trade flourished. Over time, merchants in the major urban areas of Kaesông, Pusan, and Seoul accumulated great wealth. In Seoul, huge markets developed at the city's entrances and along several mid city commercial streets in what is now the Chongro (bell street) area. The largest of the markets were near the "Great Gates," the Great South Gate, the Namdaemun (Fig. 2.1), the Great East Gate, the Tongdaemun, and the Great West Gate, the Sôdaemun. (Fig. 2.6)[8]

Fig. 2.6 Sôdaemun (Great West Gate) Sketch by A. Henry Savage-Landor, a British writer

Fig. 2.7 Seoul Grain Shop

Fig. 2.8 Market day in Ulsan, a city located on the southeastern coast of Korea

Taewon'gun

Not to fight back when invaded by western barbarians is to invite further attacks, and selling out the country in peace negotiations is the greatest danger to be guarded against.

—Engraved by Taewon'gun on *ch'ŏkhwapi*
(stone pillars) across Korea

Fig. 2.9 *Ch'ôkhwapi* erected by Taewon'gun in Pusan on the grounds of the Pusanjin castle. In response to the foreign invasion of 1871, the Korean regent Taewon'gun erected stone monuments across Korea. In addition to the bold decree to guard against attacks by the "western barbarians," eleven Chinese characters engraved in the monument dedicated the *ch'ôk hwabi* "To our descendants."

In 1864, King Ch'olchong, a traditional isolationist, died without a male heir. In the vacuum of the monarch's death, political manipulations led to the crowning of a new king—Kojong. Masterminded by the savvy Dowager-Queen, a widow of Ch'olchong's predecessor, Kojong, a twelve-year-old boy of royal linage was placed on the throne.[9] Soon after, the boy-king's father Prince Yi Hûngson followed tradition and assumed the position of regent to govern in his son's behalf. (see Fig. 2.10). Known as the Taewon'gun, (or prince-parent), the regent continued the state policy of isolationism called *t'ang p'yôngch'aek* (policy of impartiality).[10] Historian Bruce Cumings described the regent's foreign strategy as simplistic— "no treaties, no trade, no Catholics, no West, and no Japan."[11] Indicative of the Taewon'gun's conservative views, years later when confronted with a threat from the West, the de facto ruler erected monuments called *ch'ôkhwapi* (literally, stone pillars) inscribed with: "Not to fight back when invaded by western barbarians is to invite further attacks, and selling out the country in peace negotiations is the greatest danger to be guarded against."[12]

Savvy Politician

Fig. 2.10 Taewon'gun, Prince Yi Hûngson, 1820–1898

On another level, history must also regard the Taewon'gun as a remarkably crafty politician who used the anti-foreign bias to his advantage.[13] The regent, a formerly obscure prince with weak legitimacy, exploited isolationalism to win favor of the Neo-Confucian *yangban* intelligentsia who administrated the state.[14] Severe repression and persecution of Korean Catholics in 1866 drew further support from the *yangban* literati who, faced with mounting domestic problems, saw value in rallying the masses against a common enemy—Christian converts and French Jesuits missionary-priests.[15]

Western Economic Expansionism

Across the Pacific in America, the East Asian peninsula's conservative isolationist policies meant little during the first half of the nineteenth century. As early as July 1844 the United States Congress had tabled a motion to explore trade avenues with Korea.[16] In particular, New York Congressman Zadoc Pratt, the chairman of the Committee on Naval Affairs, proposed that U.S. government initiate trade with Japan and Korea. The forward-thinking proposal apparently found little support and was dropped.

The mood over Asian trade by Americans shifted during the post-Civil War reconstruction period. Following nearly five years of a war-driven domestic economy Secretary of State William H. Seward saw expansionist opportunities for America in the Pacific and heralded expanding its fledgling international mercantile empire.[17] American merchant ships free of wartime restrictions traversed the globe in search of new markets.[18]

Amiable Treatment

Even though Korea upheld a strict isolationist policy, they did deal charitably with shipwrecked westerners. Americans were first marooned off the east coast of Korea in 1855 and then again in 1865. In the 1855 incident, four crewmen of the whaling vessel *Two Brothers*, in an effort to escape an abusive captain, jumped ship and set a course on a small boat for Japan. Unfortunately, winds washed them ashore on the coast of Korea near Wonson. (see Map 2.1) The four seamen were reportedly the first Americans to set foot on peninsular kingdom. Records tell Korean villagers treated them hospitably. Orders from Seoul dictated the men be escorted to the Chinese-Korean frontier, from which they secured passage to America.[19] A better documented wreck, the *Surprise*, occurred on the northwestern coast of Korea near Ch'ôlsan in the North P'yôngan province during July 1866. (see Map 2.1) The castaways, a Captain McCaslin and his crew of seven, were fed and clothed by local Korean authorities under the jurisdiction of P'yôngan gover-nor Pak Kyusu and transported on horseback to the northern frontier and turned over to Chinese officials.[20] After the men had crossed the Korea-China border, reports told of mistreatment of the Americans by the Chinese. In contrast, the Koreans had treated the men kindly.

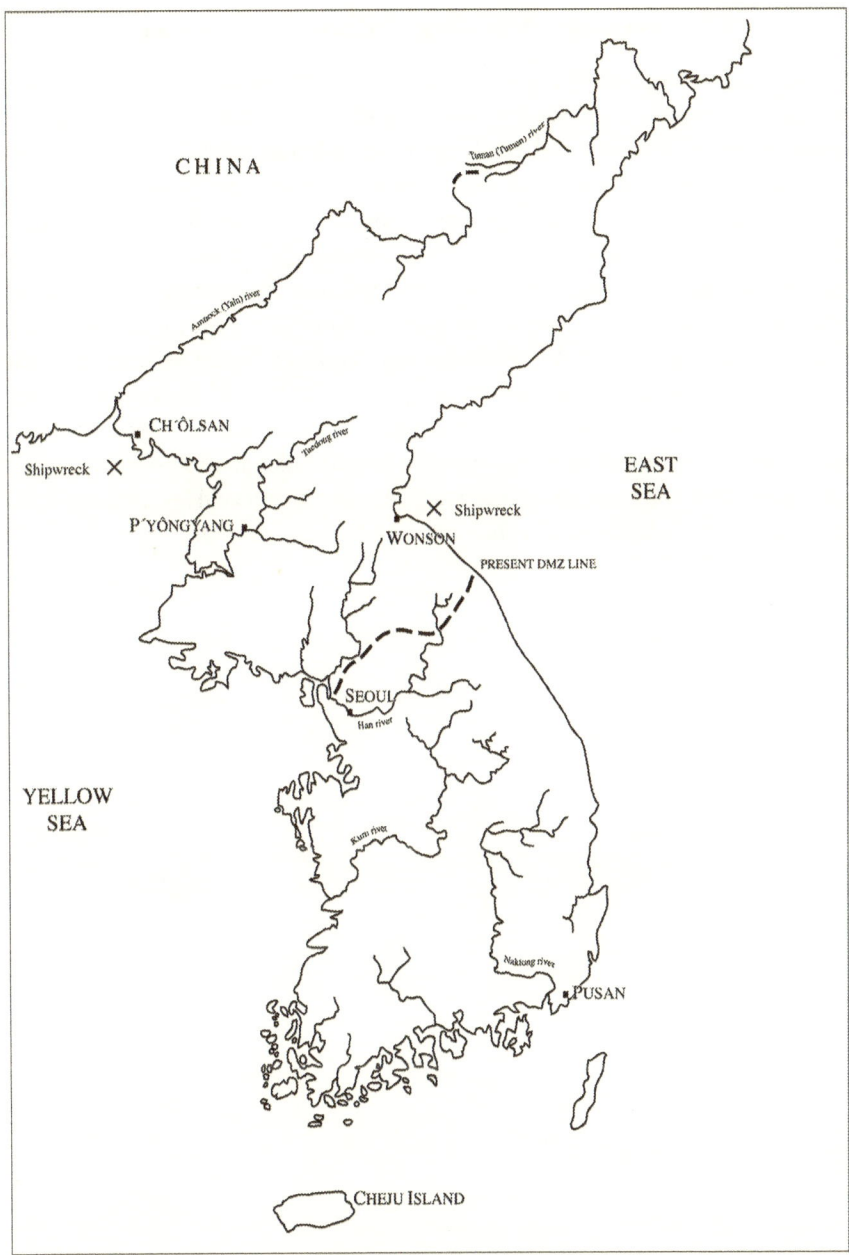

Map 2.1 Locations of mid-nineteenth century American maroonings off Korea's coasts

Shifting Policy

The previously amiable policy of treatment offered to shipwrecked western mariners shifted considerably when Anglos deliberately ventured into the Hermit Kingdom's waters and challenged the isolationism edict. A late summer American-led expedition of bold profiteers would force the Korean government to react much differently than its policy toward those previously shipwrecked. For indeed, the ruling elites would find a ship traversing their waterways a violation of Korea's dominion, in comparison to an occasional marooning. One must also acknowledge that the U.S. government did not officially endorse or condone the errant actions by a band of American-led opportunists. In fact, it seems there was little established policy or interest on the part of the United States towards trade with Korea at that time. Nevertheless, the act of a small band of westerners in the late summer would result in their own demise and unleash a response by the U.S. government that led to both military action and an eventual western-style trade agreement—topics addressed in the next chapters of this book.

Chapter Three
The *General Sherman* Incident

The populace, military, and officials heartily united in the act of killing the crew. This brave act was magnificent.
  —Joint statement by P'yôngan governor, Pak Kyusu;
    military and civilian official, Paek Nagyôn;
    and P'yôngyang mayor, Sin Taechông

Fig. 3.1 The *General Sherman*, the former *Princess Royal*

The voyage of the merchant ship, the *General Sherman*, is historically seen as the first encounter of Americans openly seeking to trade with Koreans. That the venture ended in disaster adds a significant dimension to our understanding of early U.S.-Korean business relations. Specifically, this chapter seeks to tell the "how and why's" of the voyage. Chapter Three also strives to answer questions that have perplexed many for decades. Of interest to the reader will be the perspective among the enterprising westerners who entered Korean waters in search of opportunity and profit—and stubbornly proceeded upriver even when told repetitively to leave.

The *General Sherman*

This chapter will first reconstruct the *Sherman's* early history with relevance to our story. Clouding the issue, a number of U.S. merchant ships of the mid-nineteenth century were named the *General Sherman*.[1] Fortunately, after careful scrutiny of government and private records all but one prospect was equipped with the armaments, displacement, and ownership records to be the ship in question.[2] With regard to the naming of the ship, Chart 3.1 notes the ship's multiple designations, which include the *Princess Royal*, the *USS Princess Royal*, and the *General Sherman*. The ship's renaming was the result of changing ownership during the U.S. Civil War years. The British-built *Princess Royal*, at first in use by the South's Confederacy, eventually fell into the hands of the North's navy who renamed it the *USS Princess Royal*. With the end of the war, the ship was subsequently re-christened as the *General Sherman*. Chart 3.1 and Chart 3.2 display timelines, the names of the vessel, and how the ship also changed ownership.

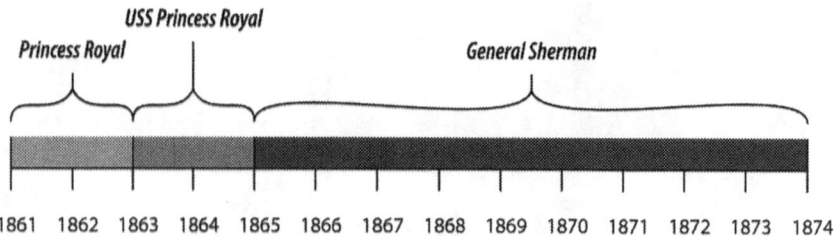

Chart 3.1 The "many names" of the *General Sherman*

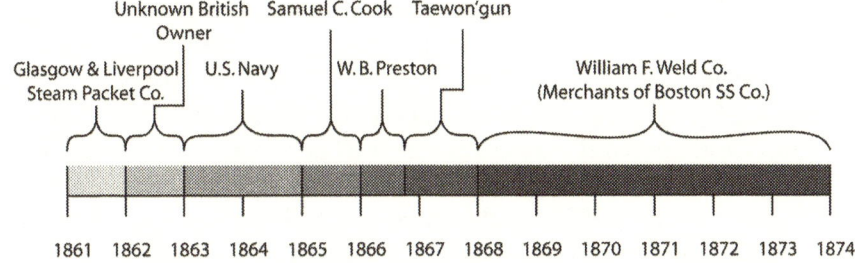

Chart 3.2 *General Sherman* **ownership, 1861–1874**

The *Sherman* in East Asia

How a de-commissioned U.S. Civil War gunship arrived in East Asia is the first of the mysteries surrounding the story of the *General Sherman*. It is thought that the *General Sherman* after serving both sides in the U.S. Civil War had made its way to Asia as part of a government effort to bolster the American presence in China. Soon afterward, it fell into the hands of Henry A. Burgevine, a self-styled American soldier of fortune. The mercenary Burgevine had boarded the *General Sherman* in 1865 with a small band of mostly Asian comrades and sailed from a port in the region to Formosa (Taiwan) to join a former Taiping rebel force. The Taiping Rebellion of 1861–1864, the largest uprising in China's history, although suppressed, still lingered among some of its participants and supporters including Burgevine. Unfortunately, for the mercenary and his colleagues the Royal British Navy captured the *General Sherman* and Burgevine died while in custody.[3] In the aftermath, Boston merchant and trader W. B. Preston acquired the ship with hopes of further expanding his business into the region.

The Crew

It is with Preston's purchase of the ship that our narrative begins in earnest during late July of 1866. Soon after, the *General Sherman* departed Tientsin, China with a cargo of cotton textiles, glassware, mirrors, tin ware, and other trade goods. On board the ill-fated ship headed for the Hermit Kingdom was a crew of nineteen. Americans included Captain Page, Chief Mate Wilson and the owner W. B. Preston. British citizens included George Hogarth, the ship's supercargo who oversaw the cargo, and Reverend Robert Jermain Thomas. The remaining members were Asian and had "dark skin."[4] One accounting of the non-Anglo crew shows that Chinese crewmember, Chao Ling feng, served as interpreter and at least two of the crew were Blacks. Sources further describe the non-Anglos as numbering thirteen Chinese and two Malays (Malaysians). Other references often tell of the crewmembers being short statured, dark-skinned Asians. The Asian trading firm of Messrs. Meadows and Co. in a 1866 letter to Her British Majesty's consul in Tientsin noted that Hogarth employed one employee from Canton to assay Korean gold and silver; Thomas employed two men from Beijing; two men from Shantung served as pilots, and the rest were Malaysians and from Southern China. There is also some speculation that when the American merchant Preston acquired the *General Sherman*, former mercenary followers of Burgevine—Malay and Chinese soldiers—stayed with the ship.

Missionary Zeal

Of the Anglos, twenty-six year old Thomas appears to have had a different agenda for embarking on the journey. A Welshman by birth, Thomas represented the National Bible Society of Scotland and had been preaching in Shanghai since 1863.[5] While in China, the missionary heard reports of the Taewon'gun's persecution of Catholics and pledged to bring the word of God to the East Asian peninsula.[6] Thomas immediately began learning rudiments of the indigenous language from Korean Catholic converts in Chefoo, China. Early in 1865, Thomas embarked on a mission to proselytize on Korea's western coast. Unwelcome on the peninsula, he was soon forced to return to Beijing via Manchuria in December of that year. Undaunted, Thomas then planned to re-visit Korea on a French warship commanded by Admiral Pierre Gustave Roze in 1866.[7] When the French fleet's departure was delayed, Thomas instead accepted an offer by the American merchant Preston to serve as the vessel's interpreter.

Trade and Plunder

In contrast to Thomas's evangelistic mission, the other westerners on board the *Sherman* were less idealistic and far more materialistic. Although the Anglo crew professed an "experimental voyage of trade and discovery," popular beliefs of the time suggested that Korea held lightly guarded ancient royal tombs containing gold coffins.[8] Supporting the argument of the ship's nefarious intent, nineteenth century writer-scholar William Elliot Griffis outright claimed that the *General Sherman* was on a mission of "plunder and piracy."[9] Griffis noted that Thomas' friends advised the youthful missionary of the expedition's suspected plans, but to no avail.[10] Joseph Longford, a contemporary of Griffis, wrote that perhaps the benefit of the doubt should be given to the owners and crew of the *General*

Sherman "whose mouths were closed by death before they had the opportunity of speaking in their own defense."[11] Nevertheless, Longford believed that their purpose was not different than Prussian merchant Ernest Oppert's infamous 1866 buccaneering attempt to locate and plunder the tomb of the Taewon'gun's ancestors. This comes as no surprise since Oppert, in "Indiana Jones" fashion, had gained great notoriety for his bold attempt to raid Korea's treasures.

In recent years, numerous historical works authored by both Koreans and Anglos have also echoed that the purported mission of the *Sherman* was to raid the treasure tombs near the city of P'yôngyang.[12] However, I think that perhaps historian Fred Harvey Harrington best summed up the voyage in broader terms indicative of American economic ventures of the time: "insistence of trade, missionary zeal, and willingness to use force."[13]

Upriver

Thus, it was in early August of 1866 that the *General Sherman* headed in the direction of the Korean port, Chemulp'o (Inch'ôn). Winds and tide then drove the ship northward. By mid-August the vessel steamed up the Taedong (River) towards P'yôngyang, the provincial capital. (see Map 3.1) The crew dropped anchor at Keupsa Gate at the border between Korean P'yôngan and Hwanghae provinces. The governor of P'yôngan province, Pak Kyusu, hearing local reports of a "warship" sent his emissary Chung Taesik to investigate the foreign presence. At the encounter, Thomas, whom the Koreans called Ch'oe Nanhôn, used an Asian crewman as an interpreter and explained to the emissary that the ship was from the land of *miguk* (United States). Moreover, that their quest was to search for Korean gold, tiger skins, rice, and ginseng. Emissary Chung informed the intruders that Korea did not trade with foreigners and that only great King Kojong could change this law; and that he and the provincial governor had no authority in such matters. The emissary then cordially offered to provide them with some provisions. The crew asked for flour and eggs. Chung gave the crew rice, beef, twenty-five chickens, and fifty eggs in the hope that the foreigners would heed his words and depart for home amiably. Chung left the ship only to see Captain Page, on Preston's urging, ignore the official's directives weigh anchor and sail upriver. Over the next several days, reinforcing Chung's plea, river village officials repeatedly tried to turn back the schooner along the river towns of Juyongpo, Songsanri, and Sahpogu. Each time they informed the crew that Christian missionaries and foreign commerce were banned in their land by the laws of the Qing Imperial Court.[14] In contrast to the official policy, commoners along the river found the ship a subject of much interest. At every stop Reverend

Thomas visited with local villagers, preached religion, and distributed Bibles.[15] At one river town alone, more than five hundred Bibles were handed out. Often, Thomas and the crew invited the curious locals onto the *Sherman*. According to one report, there were occasions when the ship was in danger of capsizing due to so many Koreans being on board. One can only speculate that despite official warnings to the crew, the apparent goodwill by the commoners encouraged them to proceed upriver.

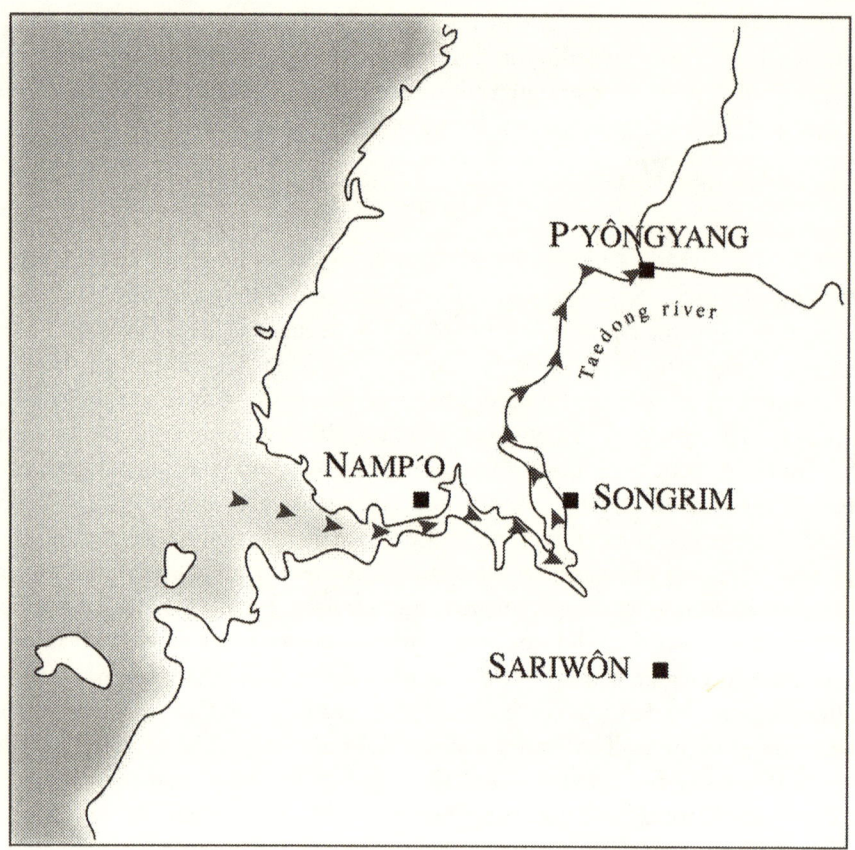

Map 3.1 Taedong River route of *General Sherman*, 1866

Soon the vessel reached Mangyungdae, down river from P'yôngyang, where rapids stopped the *Sherman* from continuing. Fortuitously, during the night it rained in the surrounding watershed, which fed the Taedong. Combined with an unusually high tide, the rainfall raised the water level. Page and his crew apparently thought that the high water was normal and proceeded over the rapids and further upriver until they reached Yangjak Island on August 27. Further enraged at reports of the foreigners' progress, Governor Pak Kyusu sent Lee Hyon Ik, the deputy commander of P'yôngyang to the vessel. Lee gave the ship an ultimatum that the King was to be informed of the foreigners' actions—ignoring orders to stay down river of the Keupsa Gate and trading with the locals—both of which were strictly forbidden.[16] When word of the foreigner's advance reached Seoul, the Taewon'gun who had anticipated some reprisals from the West for the purge of the French priests believed that this "black ship" was actually the vanguard of an invasion by the French Roman Catholics. Korean eyewitness Chông Hôijo recalled years later the de facto ruler's edict to the local officials: that if invaders did not leave at once to, "Destroy them utterly."[17] The confusion and misinformation on the ship's country of origin sealed the fate of the crew, especially since Governor Pak's report to the Taewon'gun failed to clarify, at least in the ruler's mind, that the ship was *miguk* (American). One can only speculate that if the Taewon'gun had known the *General Sherman* was not a French warship, a less aggressive stance might have been ordered. That the *General Sherman* was once a Civil War schooner, complete with armaments, only further clouded the situation.

Nevertheless, when Pak Kyusu received a firm directive from Seoul, he obediently mobilized his contingent troops to confront the foreigners. Armed with muskets and *hwajôn* (fire arrows) that could travel eight hundred feet and then explode, the troops, dressed in dragon cloud armor, a folded cloth reputedly impervious to bullets, marched past a cheering crowd to confront the invaders.[18] In tow, were several antiquated cannons.[19] Assisting the troops were a much larger force of several hundred local volunteers and some tiger hunters, men known for their courage and tenacity. Meanwhile, on the evening of August 27, with the ship anchored in the river, six of the *General Sherman* crew boarded a small blue dinghy and headed to shore. They were spotted by Deputy Commander Lee Hyon Ik, who with a band of Koreans tried to overtake and capture the dinghy. Amid a skirmish, Lee was ironically abducted and taken hostage by the westerners who returned to the protection of the *Sherman*.

Uprising

The next day the conflict escalated as locals became infuriated by word of Lee's capture. Rumors quickly spread throughout the region that the *Sherman's* crewmembers raided the shoreline, stole food, and even kidnapped some Korean women. The mood of the commoners shifted quickly from that of days earlier when the ship was but an object of curiosity. No doubt, the presence of Cantonese crewmembers did little to quell suspicions. Chinese pirates had long raided the region and their presence on the armed ship only enflamed Koreans seeking revenge.[20] That the crew of the *Sherman* confronted residents of the P'yôngan region only added to the volatility of the situation. Years later, for example, late nineteenth century westerners traveling to the area would note the "independent, manly spirit" of the region's inhabitants.[21] Scholars point out that the makeup of its society differed from the Southern provinces and made for a "more vibrant, restless population."[22]

Marooned

Back on the river, with the new threat of dropping water levels the ship's crew sought the safety of the open water by maneuvering the schooner upriver. This plan proved unsuccessful and soon fear surfaced among the crew that the ship would run aground. The *Sherman's* leaders after reviewing the options concluded only one choice was left: negotiate. With Lee Hyon Ik onboard as a hostage, several crewmembers boarded the blue dinghy and rowed towards shore hoping to parlay with the local P'yôngyang officials.[23] Shouting to the Koreans on shore, the westerners announced that they wished to talk, but only within the walled city of P'yôngyang. Since no one on the *Sherman's* dingy was fluent in Korean, the offshore negotiations failed to make any headway. Infuriated, the civilians began pelting the dinghy and the *Sherman* with rocks and threats. Unknown to the westerners, the inhabitants of P'yôngyang were renowned for their skill at rock throwing. In fact, commoners on the peninsula had at times fought as effective rock-throwers in wars. Lee Manchun, one of the rock-throwing champions, felled a schooner crewman. Soldiers armed with muskets and bows soon joined in the confrontation. Back on the river, the dingy crew now threatened by the ever-increasing barrage of insults and rocks beached their boat on a sandbar. Korean Pak Ch'ôngwun, a local drill sergeant, and his men took advantage of the situation, boarded the beached dinghy and rescued Lee.[24] It is unclear what happened to the dingy crew, but most likely they escaped in the confusion and returned to the relative safety of the *Sherman*.

Over the next few days, the crew's fate was sealed as the river level continued to drop and the *General Sherman* now lay immobile and firmly grounded on a sand shoal. Fear and panic reined among the crew, who fired cannons and rifles sporadically from the ship to keep the mob at bay. Reports told of cannon thunder echoing across the province. The fighting continued amidst a growing crowd of irate spectators. The confrontation wore on. Eyewitness Chông Hôijo recalled that as the foreigners fired their cannons a shower of deadly fragments rained down on the throng. In fact, Chông witnessed the cannon shots maim and kill several members of the crowd that had assembled.[25] In response, local troops and their supporters retreated to a safe distance on the riverbanks. This however positioned the Koreans to where their muskets and bows did little harm to the foreigners. P'yôngan province governor Pak Kyusu following orders from the Taewon'gun then commanded an all-out attack on the ship. On September 2, drill sergeant Pak Chôngwun boarded a makeshift *kôbuksôn* (commonly called a Turtle boat) to assault the *Sherman*. During the Imjin War fought between Japan and Korea from 1592–1598, Korea's most famous military leader, General Yi Sunsin, had defeated the foreign invaders with boats covered with metal sheets and cowhides. On each ship, for armament, a cannon was concealed in the front bow. This hidden cannon then fired when the vessel neared its opponent. In addition, spears stuck out of the "shell." Sergeant Pak hoped the time-proven covered naval craft would work against this new generation of foreign invaders. However as his *kôbuksôn* approached the *General Sherman* and fired, the aged Korean cannon's shots bounced off the thick skin of the modern warship. Chông Hôijo noted that a return shot from the *General Sherman* proved more effective and killed one of the *kôbuksôn* crew.[26]

Massacre

Lacking success with the *kôbuksôn* attack, Sergeant Pak Chôngwun turned to another tactic. He ordered his men to tie three boats together and loaded them up with firewood and a mixture of saltpeter and sulfur. Long ropes were attached to the boats, the firewood lit, and while adrift, guided from shore to collide with the grounded *General Sherman*. On the first attempt, the fire extinguished itself before the boats reached their target. A second array of fireboats was more successful, but the vigilant *Sherman* crew pushed them away. A third set was launched, reached the enemy, and lodged against the steamship. The American ship soon caught fire. After a futile attempt to extinguish the conflagration, the crew fearing suffocation from the stench and vapor of the burning sulfur-saltpeter concoction began to jump into the water. As the ordeal drew on, P'yôngyang troops in boats surrounded the larger ship. Little mercy was shown by those who hoped to escape the burning *Sherman* as some crewmembers tried a futile attempt to wave white flags, but most were hacked to pieces before they could reach shore.

While we find no detailed record of Page, Wilson, Preston, Hogarth, and most of the non-Anglo crew's death, there are several accounts of Thomas' end. For example, the government *Kojong Sillok* records that when the ship caught fire; Thomas and crewmember Chao Ling feng appeared at the bow and jumped into the water. Korean soldiers, who surrounded the ship, immediately captured them. When they begged for mercy, Thomas and Chao were bound in ropes and brought ashore. The angry crowd of soldiers and civilians began beating them. The missionary knelt down to say his last prayer and gave his Bible to his executioner before he was killed. In the early twentieth century, Korean Protestants, citing the *Kojong Sillok*, added first-hand accounts which noted that Thomas' slayer after reflecting on the missionary's last acts, later repented his actions and converted to Christianity. To Korean Protestants, Thomas' death supports a belief that the missionary died as a martyr bringing Christianity to Korea.

A second version of Thomas' death is Chông Hôijo's eyewitness account. Chông noted that Thomas, Chao, and two Black men made it shore. They were quickly captured and taken to a local willow grove adjacent to an ancient Buddhist stone pagoda. Soon afterwards the men were beaten to death.[27] The significance of this story is the execution site, for local lore maintains that the *General Sherman's* fate had been foreseen prior to the massacre. Moreover it was reported that the 1,000-year old Buddhist pagoda empowered the Koreans to overcome the foreign invaders.

A final version, and one promoted by William Griffis, draws on a 1884 report by Lieutenant J.B. Bernadou's, (U.S.N.). Bernadou's work contained interviews with a number of witnesses of the *Sherman* and her crew's demise. This version describes that Thomas, after escaping to the shoreline, explained to his captors the meaning of the white flag of surrender. Thomas then requested local officials return him to China. Unfortunately after a few days of imprisonment Thomas and the other survivors were publicly executed.[28] One gains from this description that his death was not at the hands of a mob, but orderly and sanctioned by the local government who acted within jurisdiction of the Taewon'gun's edict.

The significance of the multiple versions of Thomas' death reflects the viewpoints of those reporting or reviewing the incident. Protestants looked for a noble martyr, while to others, the story supported local lore and superstition. Finally, many in the region saw the deaths as justified executions, in line with the government mandate against unwelcome and hostile foreigners.

A Victorious Outcome

In the days that followed the incident life slowly returned to normal—the *Sherman's* cannons silent, its steam-powered engine cold and still. Farmers soon returned to their crops and the gentry to their scholarly pursuits and administrative responsibilities. Royal records in the *Kojong Sillok* described that many items were salvaged from the *General Sherman.* They include 2 large cannons, 2 small cannons, 3 cannon balls, 2 rifles, 162 rounds of shots and an assortment of metal pieces.[29] As a trophy proclaiming victory, the captured cannons were displayed outside the armory in P'yôngyang.[30] As sign of triumph, the *Sherman's* anchor chains hung from the P'yôngyang's East Gate Tower (see Fig. 3.2).

Fig. 3.2 P'yôngyang East Gate

Governor Pak Kyusu, ecstatic over the success of his troops, declared a celebration with food, drink, music, and dancing at the *yangban's* summer home. In addition, the governor dispatched a special messenger to Seoul with the news of the outcome. When the Taewon'gun was informed it was said that he laughed in approval and ordered that Sergeant Pak Ch'ôngwun who led the assault be promoted to a prestigious military position in the region. An indication of public sentiment following the incident was summed up in a joint statement by Governor Pak Kyusu, Paek Nagy, the ranking military and civilian official, and P'yôngyang mayor Sin Taechông. The officials' formal report pridefully stated: "The populace, military, and officials heartily united in the act of killing the crew. This brave act was magnificent."[31] Essentially, the eradication of the foreign invaders was seen as an act of national security and local pride. At least, in the minds of the P'yôngyang's officials their action towards the *Sherman's* crew was justified.

The *Sherman* Re-Born

Meanwhile, as the region rejoiced over their victory, the Korean regent had other plans for the *Sherman*. Although it was commonly thought, and is erroneously reported in most historic sources that the charred remains of the *General Sherman* lay in the river, the Taewon'gun ordered the ship salvaged and restored.[32] The government fabricated an "official" story to conceal the whereabouts of the *Sherman*. An account was circulated and made its way outside Korea that, except for its remaining metal ribs, the ship was completely burned and then the iron structure melted down. In reality, the *General Sherman* was brought south to Mangwon-jung on the Han River downriver from Seoul. The Taewon'gun, still fearful of an attack by foreigners, had begun to bolster his army and recruited the nation's top technicians to create armaments. The regent preparing for a possible invasion by a western fleet wanted a modern warship of his own. Kim Kido, a famous ship builder, was recruited to restore the damaged *General Sherman*. The reincarnated *General Sherman* was re-christened *Warship Number One(kukôn che 1 ho)*. Reports tell that on the launching day, a huge crowd of spectators gathered on the Han River bank and the Taewon'gun was seated at a perfect vantage point. The coal burning boilers built up steam and the re-born ship let out loud steam-whistles amidst cheering crowds. The ship lurched, moved a few feet, and then to the dismay of its crew buried itself in the muddy river bottom. The Taewon'gun upon witnessing the failure was said to have dropped his head forward between his knees in dismay.

Deaf Ears, Over-reaction, and Risk-takers

To summarize, misunderstanding, miscommunication, confrontation, and mystery has surrounded the voyage and demise of the *General Sherman*. Nevertheless what stands out in the narrative is how pleas by Korean officials for the ship and its crew to turn back fell on deaf ears, as the Anglo merchants pushed upriver fueled by desire of profit. In the Korean capital of Seoul, the Taewon'gun anticipating the French seeking revenge for the murder of Jesuit missionaries and their Christian converts assumed the *Sherman* was hostile. Moreover, fear and anger among the local inhabitants of the P'yôngan region further exasperated the situation. What culminated as a massacre comes as no surprise. It does however become clear that the ship's Anglo crew were risk-takers and to them Korea offered rewards well worth the risk—signs of capitalism and entrepreneurialism.

Chapter Four
Unraveling the Mystery of the *Sherman* Incident

I am really afraid the "General Sherman" is lost and that her crew have met with an untimely death—the vessel been burned and all hands cruelly murdered. It is a very sad affair.
—Mr. Wadman to the British trading firm, Messrs. Meadows and Co. in Chefoo, China 7 October 1866.

Fig. 4.1 Section of chain from *General Sherman*, East Gate Tower in P'yôngyang, c. 1930s

Early Reports

The first word outside Korea of the *General Sherman*'s demise reached Anson Burlingame, Minister of the U.S. Legation in Beijing, by way of the American Asiatic Navy Squadron. Since early in the fall of 1866, French troops, in response to the persecution and murder of Catholic priests in Korea that year, had been in the region engaged in revenge-motivated fighting with the Koreans, first on Kanghwa Island and then the on the mainland's coast and inland waterways. After weeks of fighting the French failed to take Seoul and withdrew. Upon their return to China, the French notified the Americans that the *General Sherman* had been destroyed. The dispatch included a report obtained by Reverend P. Ridel, an apostolic minister aboard the French warship *Derouniede,* from two Korean mariners. The account described the *Sherman*'s destruction and how all of her officers, crew, and passengers were murdered.[1]

To the West and the American diplomats in China, an attack on the *Sherman* and its crew was seen as unwarranted and even barbaric. This chapter unravels the mysteries surrounding *Sherman* and her crew's fate from the West's perspective. What will stand out to the reader is the difficulty Anglo officials encountered in East Asia where diplomats were unfamiliar and unskilled in the norms, policies, and customs of Korea. Moreover, the response by many was to take military action against Korea. On another level, it highlights how during this period trade and commerce between East and West faced huge barriers—culturally, ideologically, and diplomatically.

Disbelief

Early news of the *General Sherman*'s fate collected by the French also noted first-hand accounts of two French missionaries. The clergy, fearing for their lives, had been concealed in the surrounding mountains of P'yôngyang for weeks. While hiding from the Taewon'gun's forces, the priests had observed the beached *Sherman*, the fighting, and decapitation of those who made it ashore. Back in China, upon hearing news of the *Sherman* incident, members of the American legation were at first confused. The humane treatment of the crew of the American ship *Sunrise* earlier that year caused U.S. officials to initially discount the French claims of a massacre. Even in late October, S. Wells Williams, the American delegation secretary optimistically anticipated the safe return of the crew. In fact, he requested that the Chinese officials on the Korea-China frontier not mistreat the survivors and the United States would reimburse any expenses accrued.[2]

Yet, confirming the worst, a Korean dispatch to the Chinese soon surfaced and verified the destruction of a "British" ship at P'yôngyang. The report that the ship was British only further confused the American diplomats. Evidently, the Korean legation, informed by Seoul officials that Thomas was English, mistakenly assumed the *Sherman* was also of British ownership. Additional requests to the Koreans by the Americans received little satisfaction.[3] This confusion over the *Sherman's* country of origin would prove to be a major stumbling block in resolving the incident. Correspondence initiated by Chinese officials with Korea on the ship's nationality proved equally futile. In a December 11 reply to a Chinese query, the Korean government adamantly reiterated that no Americans were involved. This should come as no surprise since the Taewon'gun had long been under the assumption that the vessel was a French warship bent on revenge. Back in China, the American legation grew incurably impatient with the Sino-Korean dialogue and soon sought a third means of inquiry—this time through Japan who seemed eager to intervene. However, the fall of the Japanese Shogunate in January 1868 meant little help manifested—the new Japanese Meiji leadership was more concerned with massive domestic reforms to the island's feudal sociopolitical system.[4] In the meantime, American Secretary of State William Seward proposed a joint U.S.-French expedition to deal with Korea.[5] This received support from Rear-Admiral Henry H. Bell whose reaction was to mount a military response backed by 1,500–2,000 troops. After some thought, Seward instructed Anson Burlingame to chose a more diplomatic path hopefully with the support of the Chinese Foreign Office—one that proved ineffectual since the Chinese, who wished to distance themselves from the fiasco, denied any jurisdiction over the matter and restated their earlier position which was that the "only connection between the two countries was one of ceremonial."[6]

The Navy Investigates

Finally, after months of frustration and few answers, American officials reached a decision. It was proposed that Commander Robert W. Shufeldt of the U.S.S. *Wachusett* would be dispatched to investigate the loss of the *General Sherman*—his orders—to demand that, if there were any survivors of the schooner, they should be delivered on the deck of the *Wachusett*. (see Fig. 4.2) The commander was further directed to conduct a detailed investigation.[7] In late January of 1867, after proceeding to Korea's west coast the *Wachusett* and her crew anchored near the mouth of the Taedong. After some discussion, the Asian pilot hired to navigate the coast and inland waterways of Korea convinced Shufeldt that it was dangerous to take the vessel upriver during the winter months.

To compound the situation, Commander Shufeldt and his expedition with hopes of learning of the *Sherman's* fate came only upon isolated fishing villages with no knowledgeable or ranking officials. In an attempt to get results, Shufeldt, finally aided by the head of a local fishing village, sent a messenger to Seoul. With growing impatience aggravated by frigid winter winds, Shufeldt was left with no choice but to wait for an answer from the capital city. On the 29th of January 1867 an official, who claimed to be from the provincial capital, was presented on board the *Wachusett*. To Shufeldt's dismay the visit was not in direct response to the letter to Seoul and provided little new information on the *General Sherman* or any survivors. U. S. Navy records of Shufeldt's investigation give some insights into the probe. What stands out is how western perceptions of Korea hampered the inquiry, coupled with little cooperation offered by Korean officials.

Shufeldt's report noted:

> There are no official cities on the seaboard of the west coast; we found, however, quite a number of fishing villages, and after some unsuccessful efforts, the chief of one of these on Nien-Fo, or Cow Island, was induced to send a letter to the official of Chang-Yuen. In the meantime we endeavored to cultivate friendly feelings with the natives. They seem to be kindly disposed, but in great dread of their government, and came as little in contact with us as possible. Apparently they are a rude and barbarous people, unarmed, and the seaboard entirely defenseless…
>
> They spoke with great reserve when questioned in reference to the General Sherman, but every one of them told the same story, which they said was known all over the country, that the vessel was burned last September up the Ping-Yang [Taedong] river, and all of her people, amounting to twenty seven persons, were killed in a melee on shore by the natives, and not by order of the mandarins.[8]

Fig. 4.2 Robert W. Shufeldt, 1822–1895

The Search Continues

With the onset of increasingly hostile weather and no response to the letter addressed to the monarchy, Shufeldt departed Korea. In the weeks that followed, the veteran American naval officer with no first hand evidence and only stories from the locals attempted to piece together a possible scenerio. The commander came to believe that the local inhabitants, fearing the *Sherman* was a pirate ship, confronted the crew, set the beached vessel on fire, and murdered the crew. Moreover, Shufeldt was of the opinion that the Korean government did not sanction the massacre, perhaps due to his own experience at seeing little central government or military presence during his brief voyage into Korean waters.[9]

A year later in the spring 1868 a second ship was dispatched, the U.S.S. *Shenandoah* under Captain John C. Febiger—its mission—further investigate the fate of *General Sherman* and its crew. Like Shufeldt had experienced, Captain Febiger received little official cooperation as the ship stopped at several Korean coastal fishing villages. Better informed on the location of the *Sherman's* demise than the previous mission, the *Shenandoah's* plan was to venture up the yet uncharted Taedong. After reaching the Taedong's mouth, the *Shenandoah* steamed upriver and began quizzing the local inhabitants on information about the *Sherman*. Although most of the dialogue proved to be of little help in uncovering the mystery, Febiger did receive the official government response to the Shufeldt letter of the previous year. The letter, with few details, simply acknowledged the death of all crewmen of *General Sherman*. After charting the Taedong, Captain Febiger saw little reason to continue the search and the *Shenandoah* departed.

Back to America—What I Think Really Happened to the *General Sherman*

What is perhaps the most fascinating aspect of this story is the actual fate of the *General Sherman*. Although popularly reported as burned and sunk, the Taewon'gun had hoped that the ship when repaired and refitted might prove valuable in defending Korea against the West. As noted in Chapter Three, after the assault on the grounded ship and its crew near P'yôngyang, the fire and smoke damaged *General Sherman* was covertly towed to Seoul. After a disappointing and futile attempt to effectively refit the vessel, it lay dormant. What appears to have happened next is truly fascinating. U.S. naval archives report that sometime after the Taewon'gun restored the *Sherman* it was returned to the United States.[10] Naval records show the former warship returning to America and remaining in service as a merchant ship until it sank in a storm on January 10, 1874 near Wilmington, North Carolina.[11]

Details on how the *Sherman* came to be returned to America in the late 1860s remain a mystery. One possible answer is that the U.S. diplomatic pressure exerted on Chinese official Prince Kung, Chief Secretary of State for Foreign Affairs, and in turn, members of the Korean mission proved fruitful.[12] This would come as no surprise since S. Wells Williams, U.S. Chargé d' Affaires ad interim noted meeting with one of the Korean mission's members confidentially and obtained the particulars of the attack. Perhaps, Wells in these closed door meetings negotiated for the discreet return of the ship with the Koreans. Moreover, China's fear, expressed to Korean diplomats, that the incident might escalate and involve a joint action by the U.S., Great Britain, and France, not to mention Japan, cannot be overlooked. One can only speculate that in the months that followed the incident, some Koreans might have become more realistic in their appraisal of a potential western threat, and withstanding the Taewon'gun's stated confidence, saw merit in appeasement. On another level, the fact that the Taewon'gun allowed the return of his prized *Warship Number One*, a trophy of victory over the western barbarians, might indicate a contradiction in public policy and action. However, this move can be explained in the regent's use of isolationism and hatred of the West as a tool to solidify his power with the masses and conservative *yangban* factions. That the savvy ruler discreetly returned the vessel to the Americans was simply a way to appease growing diplomatic probes and tensions. These tactics are the mark of an astute politician and pragmatist. The Taewon'gun's attempt to refit the *Sherman* had proved a disappointment so he had little to lose in returning the ship.

American Recourse: *Sinmi yangyo*—The American Disturbance of 1871

While investigations by Shufeldt and Febiger provided scant details on the fate of the *General Sherman* to the American government the incident only reinforced the need of a treaty to protect its sailors shipwrecked on Korea's coast. One overarching U.S. concern was to protect the welfare of shipwrecked sailors, regardless of the reason why American ships were in Korean waters.

Subsequently, in May 1871 an American expedition sailed to the Asian peninsula—their purpose to secure a treaty with the Koreans.[13] In months prior, U. S. officials deliberated on a course of action—military or diplomatic. They chose to send a joint mission with Rear-admiral John Rogers, commander-in-chief of the Asiatic squadron accompanied by Frederick Low, the newly appointed U.S.

Minister to China. The men after meeting in Beijing planned on approaching their task in a fashion similar to that of Commodore Matthew Perry in Japan in the 1850s. Unfortunately, what occurred mirrored the unproductive French expedition of five years earlier. Korean shore fortifications, spotted and fired on a small armada of American naval ships, who quickly returned shots. American troops were in turn deployed in and around two forts, Kwangsôngjin and Ch'ojijin, on Kanghwa Island at the mouth of the Han River. Korean forces greatly outgunned fought to the last man. Reports tell of weaponless Korean troops, who in an act of desperation resorted to throwing gravel at U.S. troops, while others fled the attack and committed suicide rather than accept defeat.

Fig. 4.3 Aftermath of fighting, Fort du Conde, Kanghwa Island, June 11, 1871 Photograph by famed war and Asian photographer Felice Beato.

The fleet then proceeded up the Han River towards Seoul only to meet greater resistance. After remaining for three weeks, Low and Rodgers became increasingly dismayed at the prospect of negotiating a treaty. Finally, amid what was a military and diplomatic standoff with the Koreans and little hope of success, the Americans put back to sea and returned to China. To Korea's conservative leadership, the departing Americans only confirmed the virtue and morality of their strict isolationist-nativist policies. To the Americans, the failed expedition confirmed to many that this was indeed the Hermit Kingdom.

What one learns from this chapter is how ill prepared American diplomats in the region were in launching an investigation into the *Sherman* and her crew. Equally poor was their understanding of Korea with regard to East Asian foreign policies. It comes as no surprise that erroneous information on the *Sherman* incident led to the dispatch of U.S. naval ships that fared poorly in getting needed answers. After five years of futile negotiations and impasses it was thought that a stronger course of action would succeed—the outcome was however a brief but bloody military engagement on Kangwha Island. Ultimately, trade and commerce between the West and Korea would have to wait for a time when the Hermit Kingdom would agree to open its borders to outsiders.

Chapter Five
Kaehang—The "Opening" of Korean Ports to Western Trade

The nation's primal energy is in the orthodox learning; when it is full of validity a hundred perverse things cannot burst in.
— Kim Pyŏnghak, the Korean state councilor, *Kojong Sillok*

Fig. 5.1 Chemulp'o port sketch

In this chapter we will begin by exploring events that led to the softening of Korea's rigid isolationist policy. Coupled with the demise of the regent Taewon'gun and Japan's adoption and pursuit of the "gunboat diplomacy" tactics of the West, Korea gradually opened to western trade and business development. Interestingly, despite the bloody 1871 confrontation between American and Korean troops, this chapter finds the United States as the first western power to enter into formal trade relations with Korea. These relations coincided with reforms on the East Asian peninsula, reforms that, in time, made possible the rise of western style commerce.

Safe and Humane Treatment

Outside hawkish American newspaper accounts of the U.S.'s Kanghwa Island military action in 1871, America showed little interest in the *Sherman* incident or Korea in the months and years that followed. President Ulysses S. Grant did however mention the need for a treaty in his third annual message to the U.S. Congress in December 1871. The president made his intention clear stating "a desire to put an end to the barbarous treatment of our shipwrecked sailors on the Corean coast."[1] Grant instructed the U.S. Minster to China, Frederick Low, to once again seek a treaty with Korea and insure "the safety and humane treatment of such mariners."[2] Not surprisingly it appears the prevailing American viewpoint on the incident was that the *Sherman*'s crew were but the helpless victims of a shipwreck. Nevertheless, it would not be until the 1880s that the United States would enter into a trade treaty with Korea, ironically the first western nation to do so. The dynamics, which led to this western-style international treaty, are explored in this chapter and emphasize the changes that allowed East and West to bridge cultures and establish trade.

Japanese Inroads and a New Order

But first, by the early 1870s, fueled by his successes against the *General Sherman*, the French, and then the Americans, the Taewon'gun remained confident in the effectiveness of his isolationist strategy to hold off advances from the West. The expulsion of the French and Americans reconfirmed among the regent's conservative supporters the righteousness of their Neo-Confucian beliefs. This is reflected in Korean elitist Kim Pyŏnghak, a high ranking bureaucrat's statement "The nation's primal energy is in the orthodox learning; when it is full of validity a hundred perverse things cannot burst in."[3]

However, international forces soon manifested their will. In the forefront was Japan, which had for centuries engaged in limited trade with Korea. Moreover, the island nation, in the 1870s, began emulating western imperialistic tactics. After occupying Formosa (Taiwan) and the Ryukyu Islands (Okinawa), militaristic factions in Japan openly promoted the *sei-kan* campaign, the Japanese term meaning to "conquer Korea".[4] By 1871, after a series of unsuccessful attempts to

expand trade inroads into Korea, Japanese negotiations with China proved fruitful. The centuries-old traditional relationship governing diplomatic control over
Korea was dropped, the Japanese pressing China to adopt a western view of sovereignty. Thus, Japan was able to deal directly with Korea without the protective
barrier of Chinese diplomats.

Adding to the situation, in 1873, a series of political misjudgments led to the
Taewon'gun's abdication of the throne to his twenty-one year old son, Kojong.
(see Fig. 5.2) The regent had gradually alienated a number of *yangban* factions
who supported his xenophobic stance, but rejected his unorthodox domestic
reforms.[5] In addition, the Taewon'gun failed to recognize the political savvy of
his son's new wife Queen Min Myongsong, in rallying the court against him. No
longer under his father's control, Kojong was swayed by his in-laws, who formed
a strong political faction. This group, in opposition to the politics and policies of
the Taewon'gun, sought a more realistic foreign policy.

Fig. 5.2 Korean monarch Kojong in 1884. (reign 1863–1907) The twenty-fifth Chosôn Dynasty king reigned during one of the nation's most turbulent times—often fending off threats domestic and foreign; immediate family and outsiders.

Once in power, young King Kojong's curiosity grew about the world and the recent changes in China and Japan. Scholarship notes that the young monarch studied reports on "China's attitude towards the West, activities of the Western barbarianism in Peking, China's foreign trade, Japan's Westernization, the conclusion of the Sino-Japanese Treaty, the influence of Christianity, and [the] internal state of affairs in China and its comparison to conditions of Korea" all of which influenced the young ruler's perspective on foreign affairs.[6] In 1874, Chinese officials including Viceroy Li Hongzhang and Prince Kung, who as head of the

Chinese Foreign Office, convinced Emperor T'sung-chih that Russia and Japan's imperialist advances threatened the region.[7] Li and Kung reasoned that if Korea built alliances with the United States and France, it might protect the peninsula from Japan and Russia. Persuaded of the threat, the Emperor used China's elder brother role and secretly urged Kojong to build alliances with the United States. Additionally, Hung Tsun-haein, the consul to the Chinese legation in Tokyo, further influenced Kojong to sign a treaty with the Americans. Strategically, the Chinese hoped that since the United States was neither imperialistic nor perceived as a threat like the Russians and the Japanese, America might prove a valuable ally for Korea.

Kaehang—Opening of Ports

Yet before a Korean-American relationship was realized or even discussed formally, Japan had long looked across the Strait of Japan and plotted to establish a trade and business presence in Korea. With the massive reform-driven Meiji Restoration of 1868 and opening of Japan to the West, progressive Japanese envisioned Korea as a perfect market for export of manufactured goods while serving as a provider of low cost rice. Positioning itself, by 1875, the Japanese had signed a diplomatic agreement with the Russians. This document insured that Russia would not intervene if war erupted between Japan and Korea. Soon after in February 1876, Japan succeeded in signing a treaty with Korea using tactics similar to ones employed by the United States and Commodore Perry on the island people in the 1850s. Japan's envoys, General Kuroda Kiyotaka and Inoue Kaoru, boldly steamed into Chemulp'o harbor and demanded the Koreans sign the pact, as drafted, while under the threat of two Japanese warships and five transports of soldiers. Terms of the forced treaty included the opening of additional ports on the peninsula and recognized Korea as an independent state, which enjoyed sovereign rights. Japan wisely crafted this independence clause as a tactic intended to further isolate Korea from its elder brother and shield, China. Moreover, by building trade settlements on the peninsula the Japanese could keep Korea out of western control, especially that of Russian imperialists.

Meanwhile, Kojong and his supporters began a policy of domestic self-strengthening while loosening the country's isolation edict. A government reform movement called the *T'ongnikimuamun* restructured Korea's military, foreign matters, industry, trade, and education—much to the chagrin of a number of the *sadaebu* (high officials) with strong Neo-Confucian beliefs. These conservative elders protested Japanese envoys traveling the country at will and the destruction of the old order. Of interest to this work, it was P'yôngan governor Pak Kyusu who assisted in formulating an open-door policy for his country. This raises the question on why years earlier Pak, who is considered by many as a progressive thinker, had taken such a hard-line position against the *General Sherman*.[8] Several explanations surface. The first possible reason was that Pak Kyusu simply followed the directives of the Taewon'gun and did not wish to cross the oppressive regent. A second possibility is that in Pak's eyes the *Sherman* crew were but profiteers, unwilling to listen to authority and bent on plunder and piracy. Either way, Pak Kyusu in his later years recognized the need of his country to open its doors to western ideas and ways.[9]

Treaty of Amity and Commerce

There shall be perpetual peace and friendship between the President of the United States and the King of Chosen and the citizens and subjects of their respective Governments. If other Powers deal unjustly or oppressively with either Government, the other will exert their good offices, on being informed of the case, to bring about an amicable arrangement, thus showing their friendly feelings.

—Article I, Treaty of Amity and Commerce, 1882

Though Korea entered into a new modern era trade agreement with the Japanese, fundamentally little change altered its seclusion policy until the early 1880s. Under the new agreement trade was limited to a few ports and their surroundings. Outside the inroads made by Japan, trade relations with the West had remained as before. With the abdication of the Taewon'gun, rumors spread to the western world that suggested the new regime might be receptive to foreigners. Since the late 1870s, America was aggressively expanding its overseas markets, partly in response to periods of domestic economic downturns. One strategy for American manufacturers and entrepreneurs was to seek out new markets for their goods so that their businesses were not based solely on the peaks and valleys in the U.S. economy—often driven by the period's self-serving bankers and financiers.

This need to open new markets for American commerce led to pro-business government-led endeavors, which included a voyage by Commodore Robert W. Shufeldt to Asia. Shufeldt, who had led the unproductive 1867 investigation into the *General Sherman* incident, was under orders to promote American interests in the region and craft a treaty with Korea.[10] Shufeldt, wary of his earlier futile experiences with Korea, began a new round of negotiations. The commodore, after an unsuccessful attempt by supportive Japanese officials to act as an intermediary, changed tactics and sought assistance from Chinese official Li Hongzhang.

The savvy Chinese leader proved highly cooperative and even organized and presided over the negotiations. As for why the Chinese aligned with America, scholar Martina Deuchler points out that China's true aim in assisting the Americans was to strengthen its eastern flank from Japanese domination.[11] As the talks progressed, Kojong who had for eight years grown increasingly receptive to a treaty with the United States sent two diplomats to the Chinese capital Beijing. After formal diplomatic introductions the Korean envoys told the Chinese they were ready to sign an agreement with the Americans. Shufeldt who had long sought friendly relations with Korea embraced the opportunity motivated by the need to protect shipwrecked seamen and prevent another incident like that which befell the *General Sherman*. After a round of amiable negotiations, the Korean-American agreement, the Treaty of Peace, Amity, Navigation, and Commerce was finalized on May 1882. Subsequently, in the summer of that year, a similar pact was signed with Germany.[12] The Korean-American treaty heralded the growing involvement of Americans in the affairs of Korea. In turn, this opened the door for American involvement in the westernization and modernization of the peninsula—a topic fleshed out in Chapter Six.

The *Sherman* Resurfaces—Gone But Not Forgotten!

In 1885, after nearly two decades of obscurity, the *General Sherman* affair resurfaced. With the establishment of formal diplomatic relations between the two countries, the issue of liability over losses and injuries rekindled hopes of a settlement.[13] It appears from diplomatic correspondence that W.B. Preston's daughter initiated an inquiry to the State Department seeking compensation: "I consider that the Coreans treated my father not only cruelly but also unjustly and think the Government should be compelled to pay the loss. x x x x x [sic] Please send me word if I can forward any claim on the loss of his life and vessel."[14] Under the State Department mandate, George C. Foulk, Chargé d' Affaires in Korea revisited the *Sherman* incident including Ensign John B. Bernadou, U.S. Navy, 1884 accounting of the affair. Foulk's report mentioned a conversation he held with Chôn Yung Muk, an official at the Royal Hospital, a facility founded by the American missionary doctor Horace Allen. After an initial inquiry, the official spoke again with Foulk and stated he had talked to King Kojong about the incident. Kojong remarked he was very young when the event occurred and came to deplore the affair. Kojong mentioned that one of the cannons was still at P'yôngyang. More interestingly, the monarch's version as told to the American official drew attention to the actions of one Anglo—Reverend Thomas. King Kojong described the missionary as "a mighty strong man and [who] fought bravely, giving much trouble to his captor's on the shore."[15] This story is very different from the Christian view of a praying, repentant Thomas bestowing his executioner with a Bible or the account of a cowering missionary waving a white flag of submission. King Kojong concluded by noting that the governor of P'yôngan had been Pak Kyusu, "an old man, well educated, who knew something about foreign countries; he died long since."[16] Essentially, Kojong acknowledged the incident as unfortunate, but distanced himself and his government from any connection to the actions of an earlier era.

Foulk subsequently reported to his superiors in Washington, D.C. pointing out that the *Sherman*'s demise was in large part due to the "state of the times &c." This meant the Chargé d' Affaires perception followed Kojong's lead—that blame rested on an earlier time when the Taewon'gun's tyrannical power instilled terror among the masses. Thus, Foulk felt the citizens of P'yôngyang were not culpable for the incident. For Foulk, several explanations were plausible. One, the inhabitants must have feared the foreigners. Two, they believed that the *Sherman* came to avenge the deaths of the Jesuit Priests. Or Three, the Koreans felt if they did not repel the invaders they might be construed as Christian sympathizers and lose their heads to the royal executioner. Back in America and after reviewing the findings, T. F. Bayard, the Secretary of State, saw little prospect of restitution and the case was dropped. As was much surrounding the *General Sherman* and noted in earlier chapters, the ship, unknown to Preston's heirs and the U.S. government, had long since been returned to American waters.

A New Order: New Thinking

Of interest in this chapter is the thawing of Korea's isolationist policy and the rise of a new order under King Kojong in the 1870s and early 1880s. With the political demise of the Taewon'gun and Japan's bold adoption of the West's "gunboat diplomacy," trade agreements were gradually signed with the western powers. Surprisingly, as the U.S. established a legation in Korea, an early query surfaced about the fate of the *General Sherman*. However, unlike in the late 1860s, answers this time were forthcoming. In fact, top officials on both sides, looking back, attributed the unfortunate incident to conditions of an earlier time—neither party wishing to focus on the past, but on the prospects the future offered.

Chapter Six
Dawn of Capitalism, Age of Concessions

The signs of American activity, in the capital alone, are evident upon every side. The Seoul Electric Car Company, the Seoul Electric Light Company, and the Seoul (Fresh Spring) Water Company have been created by American enterprises, backed by the "liveness" and 'cuteness [sic] of the two concessionaries…and pushed along by little diplomatic attentions upon the part of the American Minister.

—Angus Hamilton, *Korea*, 1904

Fig. 6.1 Seoul Tramway c. 1903

This study now shifts forward in time by probing into the development of Korean and American business ties during the "enlightenment" or "awakening" era of the late 1800s—a time more responsive to western thought and trade. Unlike the earlier period when the isolationism dominated and few westerners dared set foot on the peninsula, by the last decades of the century numerous firsthand accounts by Anglos provide details on commercial ventures and cultural interactions as Korea opened to the West. In addition, the reader will gain from this chapter an understanding of the prevailing conditions that empowered American entrepreneurs to acquire concessions, the challenges they overcame, and the strong political and economic forces that eventually compelled them to leave the East Asian peninsula.

Missionaries

As noted, until 1882, Korean trade with the West was nearly non-existent. With the ratification of the Korean-American Treaty, the agreement heralded a growing involvement by Americans into the affairs of Korea. By the fall of 1884, Presbyterian physician Horace Allen, a doctor for the newly established American legation, arrived on the peninsula. (see Fig. 6.2) Soon after, a small cadre of

Presbyterian and Methodist-Episcopalian missionaries, too, arrived on the peninsula. In turn, this would open the door for American involvement in the westernization and modernization of the peninsula.[1]

Fig. 6.2 American missionary-doctor turned diplomat Horace Allen

Strengthening and driving American commerce's role in Korea was the union of business and Christian religious interests. Like many American ventures of the time inroads in new global markets often centered on trade and missionary zeal.[2] Moreover, in the West, capitalism has historically been seen as connected with development of the Protestant spirit.[3] During this period no organized Christian Capitalist movement or outright declaration of Christianity linked to business arose in the West, but many saw Protestantism as the religion that practiced capitalism. In fact, Max Weber's classic scholarly work argued that Calvinism supplied the moral energy and drive of the capitalist entrepreneur.[4] What does standout is that the evangelical-industrial worldview, which permeated late, nineteenth century Victorian America, was keen on the minds of the American missionaries.[5] Moreover, American industrialism funded much of the Church's missionary movement—a uniting of God and gold.[6]

Traders

Coinciding with Dr. Allen's arrival, American entrepreneurs already established in neighboring Japan entered Korea.[7] Foremost among these adventurers was Walter D. Townsend of Boston who had ventured to Japan in the late 1870s. At first, Townsend was employed by James R. Morse and the American Clock and Brass Company—a trading company that sold watches, clocks, firearms, as well as, chemicals, cast iron goods, and patent medicine cure-alls, such as "Dr. West's Vegetable Liver Pills."[8] With business-related travels between Japan and Korea beginning in 1884, Townsend soon decided to take-up permanent residence on the peninsula. Still bound to his business alliances with James Morse in Japan, the Yankee trader operated in Korea as Morse Townsend and Company. Over the years the firm primarily exported rice from Korea, while importing a wide variety of goods including millions of gallons of kerosene on behalf of oil baron John D. Rockefeller's Standard Oil Company. Like many of the early Anglo merchants and traders in the region, Townsend took an Asian wife (from Japan). This union over the years proved advantageous since it gave him insights and links to Japan, which served as his primary trade connection.

Fig. 6.3 Korean city streets, Seoul in 1890s

Sights and Sounds

The first Anglo diplomats, missionaries, and traders entered Korea through the port of Chemulp'o (now part of modern Inch'ôn), which was within proximity to the capital, Seoul. Chemulp'o was an old fishing village that served as the region's primary port. Accounts by this first wave of Anglos to Korea as well as their impressions and experiences are well documented and add dimension to this study. The Anglos, for example, found the port's narrow streets less than desirable in sight and smell as open ditches on either side of the road flowed with sewage and domestic waste. Flanking the streets and meandering passages were rows of Korean commoner's homes, most one room mud and stone structures with thatched roofs. With their low doors, occupants had to duck to enter, the windows were covered in paper instead of glass. In outward appearance, many Koreans seemed akin to the destitute of London or New York. This is significant because the sights and sounds of urban life confirmed biased Anglo perceptions that Korea was indeed backwards and undeveloped by western norms. In actuality, the inhabitants lived lives of reasonable comfort with few going hungry or cold—this could not be said of the poor of Northern European and American cities.[9]

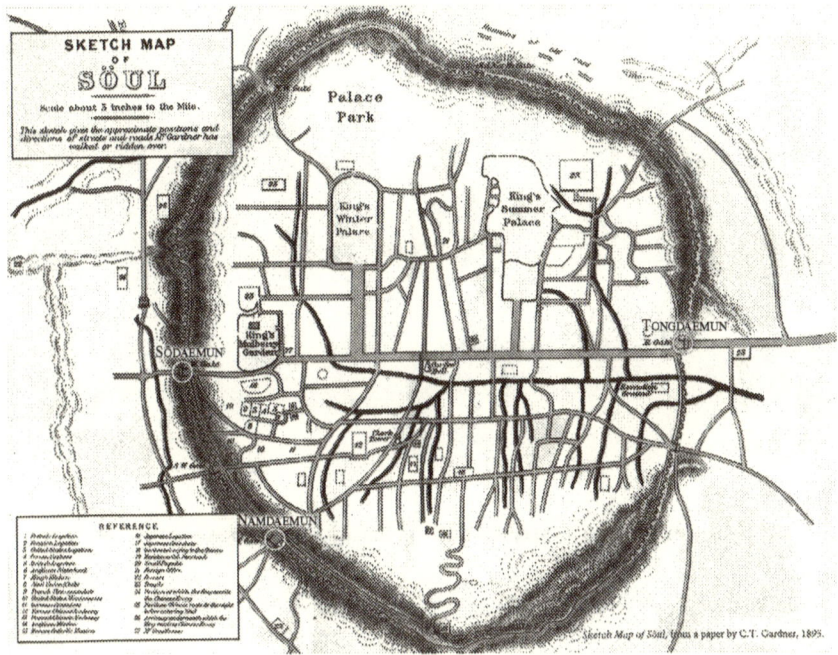

Map 6.1 Anglo Sketch Map of Seoul, 1895 (The city's three principle "Great Gates" have been highlighted)

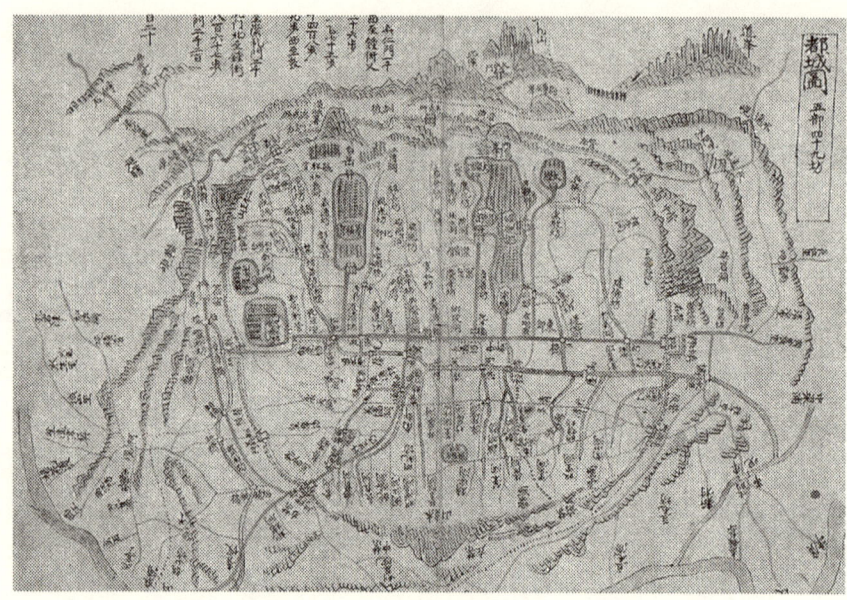

Map 6.2 Korean street map of Seoul, nineteenth century

In neighboring Seoul, inland a day's walk from Chemulp'o, early traders and visitors found a walled city with formidable gates, locked each night at nine o'clock with the sounding of the *Boshin* bell, an ancient ten-foot high bronze bell housed in a pavilion near center city. (see Fig. 6.4) With ancient battlements and royal palaces, Seoul was located in a picturesque valley surrounded by hills. (see Map 6.1 and 6.2) Like Chemulp'o, the streets meandered. However, unlike Chemulp'o, the Korean capital city had legions of nobles and *yangban* statesmen dressed in elaborate garb. Ambling with their entourages, the elites traveled about in palanquins carried by sturdy bearers of lower class.[10]

Fig. 6.4 Seoul's *Boshingak* (bell pavilion) dates back to the reign of King T'aejo, founder of the Chosôn Dynasty. The pavilion located in the heart of the old city was destroyed and rebuilt numerous times over the centuries. Each morning and evening, its rings signaled the opening and closing of Seoul's gates.

Fig. 6.5 Korean-style palanquin with its bearers and passenger

Outside Seoul's role as the administrative and bureaucratic center of Korea, the demands of the monarchy necessitated legions of retainers, eunuchs, politicians, sorcerers, blind diviners, concubines, court musicians, and artisans. As noted in Chapter Two, trade in Seoul centered outside the Namdaemun, the Great South Gate, and in several other commercial districts. Here rice, Korea's basic trade commodity was exchanged for other goods. Merchants after a day of haggling over prices often sat next the city's South or East gates in *chumak* (vine tents), sipped local *makkôlli* (Korean rice wine), and snacked on spicy side dishes.

Accounts by the western missionaries and traders also tell of life among the masses. Often described was the plight of women of low and common birth who labored ever busy—rearing children, pounding laundry in nearby streams, and cooking meals. (see Fig. 6.6) In contrast, women of the elite class lived lives controlled by strict norms and Neo-Confucian tradition. For example, unlike the lower classes, *yangban* women were only free to ventures outside the inner sanctuary of their walled and gated homes, one hour before dark. And then, tradition demanded that their faces be covered in an elaborate hooded garb, or transported in closed palanquin. (see Fig. 6.7)

Fig. 6.6 Korean women commoners

Fig. 6.7 Korean woman of elite status with traditional *ch'ône* (cloak)

With the opening of Korea, foreign influence was soon seen in port towns of Chemulp'o, Wonson, Pusan and the capital city, Seoul. Telegraph lines, government hospitals, and administrative buildings meant western thought and modernization were making inroads. Although inland, away from a growing western influence, little changed as farmers tended their small plots of land and cultivated cash crops that included ginseng.

Fig. 6.8 Korean farmer-commoner

Nevertheless, what outsiders had once seen as the Hermit Kingdom was quickly becoming the chessboard of foreign imperialists including China, Japan, and Russia. Internally, factions among the Korean elite and commoners clashed over the path the nations should take. Essentially, the decade from 1884–1894 saw both domestic revolt and increased threat from outside Korea's borders.

Early Mining Interests

As Korea moved into the last decade of the century, progressive reforms called the *Kabo Kyôngjang* manifested in hundreds of new regulations that impacted the domestic postal system, quarantine and military issues, and gold mining, an exclusive domain of the monarch.[11] In addition, China's on-going efforts to thwart outside business interests evaporated with the Chinese military's defeat in the brief East Asian conflict—the Sino-Japanese War of 1894–1895. Capitalizing on the recent changes, Dr. Allen, now head of the U. S. Legation advised King Kojong that enlisting American capital through concessions might be a strategy for increasing the U.S. government's interest in the peninsula in an attempt to reduce ever-growing Japanese domination.[12] Korean concessions at this time, like those in China and the region, were essentially a business favor granted by the conceding government to another nation's diplomats.

The substantial profit and status of these enterprises caused considerable infighting among representatives of rival nations in Korea, not to mention the prestige among the vying nations for selection of a concession.[13] With this in mind, Dr. Allen strove to gain concessions through vigorous lobbying efforts. In 1895, Allen's efforts proved successful with the Imperial Household granting the concession for the Unsan mining district to James R. Morse, an American who was president of the American Trading Company of New York and Yokomama, Japan (the former American Clock and Brass Company).[14] Upon the formal requests approval in April 1896, Morse controlled the rights to gold production for over 500 square miles in what is today part of North Korea's North P'yôngan province.[15] Morse's twenty-five year agreement stipulated that twenty five per cent of the net profits were to be paid to the Imperial Household.[16]

Morse, although not originally seeking a mining concern, nevertheless traveled to New York City to raise capital and rendezvoused with an associate Leigh S. J. Hunt, a debt-ridden former Seattle newspaperman.[17] It is in New York City that the men met Henry Collbran. British-born, but a naturalized citizen of the states, Collbran had traveled to America in 1881 and found employment in the railroad industry, first in the Southeastern U.S., and then in successful Colorado ventures in Denver and the Cripple Creek mining region. (see Fig. 6.9)

Fig. 6.9 Henry Collbran, 1852–1925

In the summer of 1896, Collbran, after severing his Colorado railroad affiliations, set off on a vacation to his native London with a quick stop in New York City. Morse and Hunt eager to find backers persuaded Collbran to accept a one-thirds option on the Unsan gold-mining concession.[18] Collbran returned to Colorado where his family still resided, hired a mining engineer, and headed to Korea. Although winter weather meant bitter winds, frozen ground, ice and snow, Collbran was soon on the East Asian peninsula trekking across the Unsan mining district, the massive 500 square mile concession. The team determined the presence of large low-grade quartz veins, but family sources tell of how Collbran lamented over the prospect of training Koreans in western mining technology and the excessive cost of transportation.[19] Collbran promptly dropped his options and accepted a loss of $10,000 for the preliminary investigation.[20] Morse, likewise, felt Koreans could not be taught the required mining skills and the operation would then require the recruitment of costly Cornish miners from England. Morse, sold his rights to the remaining partner Leigh Hunt, who in contrast optimistically felt Koreans would learn the new technology. Hunt, for his efforts and foresight, saw the venture, the Consolidated Mining Company, grow into the richest gold mine in Asia (see Fig. 6.10).[21]

Fig. 6.10 The Consolidated Mining Company mill and mine, Unsan region.

No sooner had Collbran returned to Seoul than a new opportunity arose. Morse whose original interest in Korea had actually been a railroad concession, again benefited from the efforts of Dr. Allen who skillfully secured the rights to the nation's first railway from Chemulp'o (Inch'ŏn) to Seoul, a twenty-six mile stretch.[22] Morse, not wishing to anger his Japanese trade partners who also sought the concession, wisely asked Collbran to handle the project.[23] After accepting, Collbran returned to Denver and was back in Korea by October of 1897 with a new junior partner Harry R. Bostwick of San Francisco. Completed in a year and at a cost of $1.5 million, the railway was constructed in standard gauge, which meant American-built Pullman cars traversed the rails in contrast to Japan's railways with narrow-gauge track and European compartment-style cars.[24] This would set the standard across the peninsula. Despite labor issues with the Japanese skilled laborers, who often walked off the job on the slightest provocation, the project opened the door to future opportunity for Collbran and his colleague Bostwick. Near completion of the project, Morse, whose major business and trade interests were in Japan, sold his rights for the Seoul-Chemulp'o line to a group of Japanese businessmen. Regardless of the rail line's eventual ownership, to many, the new railroad represented Korean *progress*, a feeling even echoed in the Korean nationalist newspaper, *Tongnip Sinmun* (*The Independent*). The progressive Korean paper remarked with pride that the sound of the train shook the ground and sounded like thunder.[25] Equally proud of the accomplishment that railroads brought was American missionary Horace G. Underwood who remarked that as the railways soon crossed the peninsula, patrons rode in cars made in Wilmington, Delaware, drawn on a Baldwin locomotive, upon steel rails from the Carnegie works, nailed to Oregon ties, and secured with American spikes.[26] Ironically, Korean railroads were one concession that would stay firmly in the control of the Japanese.

Edison, Electric Lights, and Electric Trolleys

The introduction of new technology on the peninsula first stemmed from the mid-1880s when King Kojong contracted the Edison Light Company to electrify the Royal Kyôngbok Palace. Completed in 1887 by technicians from Thomas Edison's laboratory, generators powered the palace's lighting and operated electrical devices to the king and court's amazement. (see Fig. 6.11) For example, an engineer on the project, Henry English, once remarked that while wiring the palace, as a lark to entertain onlookers, the technician announced he would kill the frogs in the palace pond and then revive them. With a crowd watching, English wired and briefly shocked the pond water, paralyzing the helpless frogs. Then, after turning off the electric circuit, the stunned frogs slowly regained consciousness and resumed swimming, while wide-eyed Koreans bowed to Henry English in amazement.[27] Several years later, in 1893, electric plant was built for the Changdôk Palace, and thereafter a third official structure was electrified. Reports of the time by Dr. Allen told that the incandescent lights were most often used for court meetings held during the evening hours.

Fig. 6.11 The hexagonal Hyangwon chông, a pagoda within Royal Kyôngbôk Palace complex, was the first structure illuminated with electricity in Korea.

By the late 1890s, the Korean monarch, now self-elevated to official title of emperor, sought to modernize Seoul with electricity and telephone service; Kojong idealistically hoped that the new technology would strengthen his country economically. Plans were made and the Seoul Electric Company (Hansông chôn'gi hoesa) was formally established. In the meantime, a Korean official visiting Washington, D.C. witnessed firsthand the horse-drawn rail system converted to electric trolley cars. Upon the diplomat's return to Korea he convinced the Emperor to build Asia's first streetcar system, and like in the U.S. capital, one powered by electricity. Collbran and Bostwick upon hearing news of the concession pressured Dr. Allen to broker the deal. To avoid losing the deal to others vying for the concession, the cagy U.S. government official arranged for the partners to meet with Korean officials at Allen's residence to insure secrecy and hopefully, success. When the contract was signed in February 1899, for the joint rights to operate the system, Allen triumphantly boasted it was his finest piece of work accomplished in a decade and a half on the peninsula. Like with the Seoul-Chemulp'o railroad project, the Americans mobilized quickly. By the spring of 1899 streetcars of the Seoul Electric Car Company were running over an initial short stretch of track near one of the royal palaces to the tomb of the Kojong's assassinated wife, the late Queen Min.

As month's passed, new tracks were laid. (See Fig. 6.1 and 6.12) Interestingly, according to the Collbran family records, the monarch although proud of the project and in possession of his own private car, never rode the system.[28] In fact, at the official opening of the trolley line, Kojong agreed to sit in his car, but would not let it move.

In conjunction with the trolley line project, electric lighting, too, began sprouting up to illuminate the rail lines, stores, and homes of high-ranked officials. Each light bulb was ten watts and a monthly fee of 1.6 *Won* (the price of twenty five pounds of rice or three day's wages for skilled worker) was charged for each light.[29] Meanwhile by 1900 the Namdaemun (Great South Gate) to Sôdaemun (Great West Gate) line was completed. Fare varied according to distance and class on the trolley, with the area in the middle of the car near the windows designated as first class and the rest of the car as second class.[30]

Fig. 6.12 Seoul Tramway with front-mounted innovative "People Catcher"

Stories about how Koreans became accustomed to the streetcars abound, most about educating the populace in western-style mass transit. For example, people failed to yield to oncoming trolleys. This led to accidents. One solution was the installation of "people catchers" on the trolleys. (see Fig. 6.12) Other less life threatening challenges included informing Koreans not to follow common etiquette and remove their shoes prior to riding the streetcar. In the first days of the trolley line's operation some Koreans were surprised to find that their foot apparel was not at the other end of the line. Over time, the streetcar system became extremely popular among Koreans in spite of its high fare relative to an average worker's wages. Korean scholar Homer Hulbert remarked that by 1905 the heaviest traffic was on stone-fighting days, a traditional amusement that drew thousands of spectators near the city gates. On these occasions an estimated 34,000 riders, double the daily average, used the Seoul system.[31]

Mounting Debt

Collbran's efforts on the Asian peninsula were not without challenges. Emperor Kojong's reluctance to grant additional concessions for a modern waterworks and additional mining endeavors were compounded by Japanese and Russian maneuvering for control over the peninsula. Furthermore, the emperor whose income was eroded by poor money management, widespread corruption, numerous modernization projects, and ever-increasing government expenses was constantly pressed for cash. This meant that by 1900 when the Boxer Rebellion erupted in China, Kojong seeing the need to bolster his army agreed to issue an often discussed "Greater Concession" for the entire peninsula, excluding pre-existing arrangements like Hunt's Oriental Consolidated gold mine in Unsan. For the new mining rights, Kojong demanded a loan of $5 million, but the turmoil and instability of the Chinese rebellion frightened away any prospective western investors. Meanwhile, Kojong's debt grew to Collbran's firm for the construction projects in Seoul. By 1901, the emperor owed Collbran and Bostwick in excess of $800,000, secured with mortgages on the electric and streetcar companies with the partners also holding $330,000 of Kojong's cash in a private bank. One remedy Collbran sought was a construction project for the Russians in Port Arthur. Terms of the prospective project included selling the electric facilities and trolley to the Russians, eager to gain more interests in Seoul. Collbran and his partners decided against this plan since the streetcar system produced $2,000 in profit per month. The American partners even tried pressuring the State Department to dispatch the U.S. Navy to occupy a Korean port and force Kojong to pay up.

Gap-Filers

Aside from the debt issue, Collbran and Bostwick did press-on with their business ventures such as expanding the electric power plant to meet an ever-growing demand for electricity and adding additional streetcars routes. They also looked for more innovative pursuits. This included building the first film theater in Korea. American Elias Burton-Holmes had first introduced cinema to the Korean royal family in 1899. Soon afterwards, Collbran and his firm hoping to hold valuable, skilled workers began showing films as an employee perk. The success of private film screenings led Collbran to go into the movie theater business. Beginning in June 1903, Collbran began luring moviegoers into a makeshift theater at the Seoul Electric Company Machine Warehouse near the Tongdaemun (Great East Gate); the show's admission fee was equal to three cents.[32] Shrewdly on Collbran's part, moviegoers were drawn in from the crowds of disembarking passengers of the trolley line. To the mutual benefit of both enterprises, the movie audience then viewed screen ads promoting the excitement of streetcar line. It would come as no surprise that by 1905, the theater known throughout Seoul as the Tongdaemun *hwaldong sajin* (motion picture) had become a popular attraction.

Fig. 6.13 Tongdaemun, the Great East Gate with trolley tracks and overhead electric power lines.

Fig. 6.14 Seoul Offices of the Collbran-Bostwick Development Company

Like the cinema, Collbran overtime sought out other diverse enterprises. As with most entrepreneurs, he saw opportunity and then set out to meet a public demand. In Seoul, these business endeavors grew to include the telephone franchise, a coin mint, and a bank; all businesses managed from the stately Collbran-Bostwick Development Company building. (see Fig. 6.14) For many, the tower of the Collbran-Bostwick building, complete with a flagpole displaying the Stars and Stripes, symbolized America's presence in Korea. The tower's time clock even served as the official western-style timepiece for the city.

Collbran's business interests proved to be wide-ranging. One unusual example was when Emperor Kojong desired a "navy." As a favor, a high-ranking government offical asked Collbran to review a stack of submitted bids for a naval vessel. The savvy businessman consented but also submitted his own bid to those already under review. Family stories tell of Collbran winning the selection due to an additional feature, a searchlight. To fulfill the contract, the American quickly purchased a Chinese Customs cruiser and added the lighting. The family story concludes with mention that the Emperor Kojong appointed some twenty Korean Admirals for his new "navy."[33]

More Challenges

Unfortunately, the constant pressure exerted on the monarchy and some heavy-handed diplomatic maneuvering pursued by Collbran and Bostwick regarding the outstanding debt took its toll. Coupled with growing tensions among some Koreans, open protests erupted. In October 1903, a three-day riot was staged. In the frenzy, an American manager of the electric firm was killed and property destroyed. To compound the unrest, in January 1904, an accident with a *jin-rikisha* driver who refused to yield to an oncoming streetcar was killed when the much larger vehicle's icy brakes failed to stop in time. A crowd gathered at the accident site and turned over the streetcar requiring a platoon of U.S. Marines to break up the near riot.[34] A month later, after waiting three years to resolve Kojong's debt issues the onset of the Russo-Japanese War on February 8, 1904 forced the ruler into action. Several days after the Japanese battle fleet steamed into Inch'ôn harbor and troops landed in mass, one of the emperor's chief negotiators accompanied by William Sands, diplomat-turned-advisor to the ruler, met in secret at Collbran's home to settle the debt.[35] Terms reached included a one-time payment by Kojong of $375,000, and an equal partnership in the electric company, renamed the American Korean Electric Company.[36] A construction contract was also signed awarding Collbran's firm the waterworks project with an agreement that the Korean Customs commissioner compensate the Americans $100,000 annually for ten years. Finally, to settle the remainder of Kojong's debt, the negotiators made provisions that gave Collbran's firm a broad monopoly over Korea's mineral resources to extend ten years after the war ended.

Change Brings New Opportunity

With the end of the Russo-Japanese War in 1905, Korea, now the pawn of the Japanese imperialistic control was forced into perhaps the darkest chapter of modern Korean history. Undaunted Collbran and Bostwick launched a number of ventures including expanding the electric system and beginning construction on the modern waterworks. Moreover, a day after the war ended Collbran's son Arthur a 1901 graduate of the Colorado School of Mines began a trek north to the Kapsan district in Ryangyang province. Here in the northern region of Korea bordering China, a potentially massive copper mining operation extended over at least 1,000 square miles. Upon the younger Collbran's return to Seoul, the Collbran and Bostwick Development Company notified the Korean government it wished to execute its contract. The Japanese officials, now essentially in control of the country, refused the demand. Still, over the next two years the American entrepreneurs pressed forward with their utility projects, especially the new water filtration plant. They also branched into gold mining by assuming control over the British concession in Suan, southeast of P'yôngyang in Hwanghae province.[37]

In 1908, after years of international negotiations involving the American, British, and Japanese governments a compromise over the Collbran-Bostwick interests in Korea was reached. To gain the massive Kapsan mining operations, Collbran and Bostwick under terms of an agreement sold their newly completed $1.5 million waterworks to a British syndicate, while the Japanese purchased the Americans' half interest in the electric company for $620,000. In addition, $150,000 was paid to the remaining partner, the now deposed Kojong. This resulted in the Japanese holding a monopoly on public transportation, electricity, and gas in the Korean capital. The former American Korean Electric company was subsequently renamed Kyôngsông (Seoul) Electric Company (KEC).

Content with the profits, Harry Bostwick returned to San Francisco where the businessman became involved in the reconstruction of the city in the wake of the infamous earthquake and fire of '06.[38] Meanwhile, in April 1908, Collbran incorporated a new mining firm, the Seoul Mining Company. Interestingly, the company was headquartered in Denver, Colorado; where among its largest stockholders was his son Albert's father-in-law, beer baron Adolph Coors. With his three sons overseeing daily operations of the two profitable Korean mining operations, the elder Collbran frequented his home in Denver, before eventually returning to his native London where he lived out the remainder of his life in leisure. (see Fig. 6.15) The Kapsan copper mine amid constant hampering by Japanese officials was sold to the Kuhara Mining Company in 1915 for $1.5 million.[39] The Suan operation lasted until 1924 when the ore played out; whereby the mine was closed as were the last of the Collbran holdings on the peninsula.[40] Henry Collbran died the next year at age 73.

Fig. 6.15 Henry Collbran home. Denver, Colorado

A Summary

Conditions by the late 1880s allowed American missionaries and traders to make inroads, figuratively and literally into Korea. They in turn served as a vanguard for American business interests on the peninsula. Paramount was missionary-doctor turned diplomat Dr. Horace Allen's influence with the court and monarch. For nearly a decade, Dr. Allen championed American interest in Korea and provided invaluable support for American entrepreneurs in obtaining lucrative concessions. This chapter highlighted the achievements of the leading concessionaires—Henry Collbran and his colleague, Harry Bostwick. What stands out is how these entrepreneurs took bold risks, overcame challenges, and profited. Moreover they constantly sought out new opportunities and served as gap fillers whether it was in supplying electric lighting to businesses in Seoul or ventures like a motion picture theater.

Chapter Seven
Early Korean Entrepreneurialism

The employees are largely Koreans, both in the powerhouse and on the line everywhere. It is the unanimous opinion of the Americans who operate the road, that the Koreans make competent hands in every department of the works. This is a striking testimonial…in settling the question whether, as so many foreigners think, the Korean is capable of attaining proficiency in the field of applied science.
—Homer B. Hulbert, *The Passing of Korea*, 1906

Fig. 7.1 Bird's eye view of Seoul trolley from atop the Namdaemun in the 1900s. Koreans carefully watched the introduction of western style business ventures and technology to the peninsula.

Chapter Seven shifts from the earlier chapters' narrative accounts to a discussion on the roots of early Korean entrepreneurialism and the rise of capitalism. On the former of these two topics, I attribute several influential forces to the rise of Korean entrepreneurialism. First, Koreans learned by working with Anglos such as Henry Collbran. As workers, Koreans quickly acquired proficiency in business and technical skills in the employ of western ventures. Secondly, opportunities abounded for Koreans as small business owners in the environs of the rural mining operations and urban trolley and train lines. One another level, a powerful influence discussed in this chapter includes the promotion of business by the Protestant church and its western missionaries. Missionaries preached progress, self-reliance, and a gospel of social capitalism.

With regard to this chapter's second topic, Korean capitalism, lively debate has preoccupied both Korean nationalist historians and a number of western scholars. Of relevance, one will gain considerable insights into characteristics cited today as factors contributing to the success of contemporary Korean entrepreneurial businesses like Samsung, Hyundai, and LG, and that surfaced in the late nineteenth and early twentieth century.

Roots of Korean Entrepreneurship

Henry Collbran and his ventures provided much needed services and western technology to Korea. Interestingly, Collbran's early opinion of the Korean worker was less than flattering, echoing a stereotype that they were lazy and non-trainable. That opinion changed, for years later in a brief submitted to the U.S. State Department, Collbran remarked that he had erred in failing to appreciate the Korean worker.[1] He, like fellow American entrepreneur Leigh Hunt found them highly employable. Collbran recognized in Koreans hard-working, ambitious traits, which were harnessed in mining ventures, the streetcar line, electric power facilities, waterworks, a coin mint, and even the first cinema. In contrast, to lessons learned in Collbran's first Korean venture (the Seoul-Chemulp'o railway) and the subsequent early operation of the trolley line, the concessionaire came to realize that using Japanese technicians and laborers proved costly. Collbran recognized that work depending on the Japanese was often plagued with incidents designed to impede smooth operations. It was hoped that the discouraged American owners would then sell the business to the Japanese. In one instance, after several trolley accidents led to an electric trolley car burning and an attack on the powerhouse, the Japanese crew walked off the job and demanded their nation's soldiers stand guard. Instead, Collbran's solution was to bring in additional help from the West with some of those recruits including gun-toting burly

San Franciscans to provide protection. To further man the operation Collbran employed an ever-increasing number of competent Koreans. Collbran's choice of Koreans over Japanese speaks volumes—the American found the domestic workforce at par with skilled sojourners and without fear of strike or threat of walkouts.

Fig. 7.2 Seoul Electric Company official Yi Ch'ae Yôn (leaning on the sledge hammer) with Dr. Horace Allen (the tall gentleman with glasses and the derby) at the September 12, 1898 dedication of the Seoul electric streetcar project.

Joint Ventures and Korean Small Businesses

It is noteworthy that most of the Collbran enterprises were in fact joint ventures. For example, the Seoul Electric Company's early Korean organizers Yi Kûnbae, Kim Tusûng and Yi Ch'ae Yôn allied with Collbran in the construction and management of the project. (see Fig. 7.2) Likewise, for the smooth operations of ventures as with the electric company, Korean involvement proved invaluable with many coming from educated *yangban* and *chungin* lineages. For instance, as described in Chapter Two, those of the *chungin* status once held hereditary position in the Chosôn society as technocrats, translators, interpreters, scribes, and professionals. No doubt these workers in the employment of Collbran learned much about western business and new technology. Moreover, commoners and the merchant class entered the market to support the mining, construction, and public work projects. For example, Unsan gradually developed into a booming frontier town in the middle of the North Korean virgin forests. It soon had its own power station and hospital. Likewise, the mining towns of Kapsan and Suan had their own Korean tailor shops, noodle shops, tinsmiths, and dozens of other service-oriented businesses. One example of Koreans entering the market as shop-keepers includes Pak Sûng Ik (Park Seung-jik) who by 1896 had opened a small shop in the Paeokae (Baeokae) district of Seoul. From these humble beginnings his descendants would build the enterprises into the Doosan Group—one of South Korea's largest conglomerates.

These predominately Korean-run enterprises fanned the flames of capitalism and saw the entrance of many into entrepreneurial ventures. In fact, the capacity to seek out opportunity is the starting point of entrepreneurship.[2] Culturally, these Korean small businesses drew upon the ethnic resources of working long hours, mobilizing unpaid family labor, nepotism, and employer paternalism and built upon traditional concepts of that included *anchông* (stability or security) and *poram* (worthiness).[3]

Fig. 7.3 The Tul Mi Chung reduction plant (Suan region). Like other sites across peninsula, Korean-run small service businesses and shops supported the daily needs of hundreds of workers.

Fig. 7.4 Shopkeepers throughout cities such as Seoul, Pusan, Kaesông, and P'yôngyang catered to the needs of their customers.

Fig. 7.5 Shoe store. Traditional footwear was of simple design and usually made of felt, hemp, cloth, and animal hide.

Fig. 7.6 Korean youth candy vendor in Chemulp'o near the train station. By the early 1900s, signs of capitalism sprouted up across Korea.

Fig. 7.7 *Kimch'i* pot shop. Shops range of goods became quite extensive. Some products like *kimch'i,* perhaps the most popular of indigenous foods, created great demand and warranted its own "specialty shop."

God and Mammon

Thus do commerce and the Church go hand in hand, here [in Korea] *as elseware, in forwarding His kingdom and spreading abroad the knowledge of the Prince of Peace.*
—Horace G. Underwood, *The Call of Korea,* 1908

Fig. 7.8 Horace G. Underwood

Instrumental in fostering the development of Korean business and capitalism was the work of Protestant missionaries in Korea. To some Koreans, Protestantism was a path to national salivation, economic self-strengthening, and progress. By the 1890s, Dr. Allen by then head of the American diplomatic legation in Seoul, and others, began stressing the vibrancy of western technology, capitalism, and civilization over Korean orthodoxy. Essentially, the changes and reforms to the Korean socio-economic landscape coupled with Church policy of egalitarianism impacted those of the lower and commoner classes, not to mention women and the oppressed such as the *paekchông* (butchers and meat handlers). Many Koreans hindered for eons from social and economic mobility by a rigid social stratification embraced Protestant teaching, western education, and western thinking, as they searched for opportunity in the newly restructured society.

Within this climate of change, the missionaries specifically targeted merchants, lower level government officials, clerks, technicians, and professionals. It was hoped that members of the newly emerging middle class with some financial means would form the backbone of the Korean Protestant church. This group of Koreans worked for businessmen like Collbran during the week and attended church on Sundays—church services that saw poverty as sinful, and praised worldly gains. In other words, weekdays and work served as opportunities for ambitious Koreans to learn western business and technological skill, while Sunday sermons drenched them with the missionaries' capitalist gospel.[4]

Adding to the dynamics, American industrialism also funded much of the Church's missionary movement—a uniting of God and gold.[5] For example, British-born Horace Grant Underwood who had grown up in upstate New York came from a religious and prosperous business family. Underwood's older brother John grew the family ink manufacturing business into the highly successful Underwood Typewriter Company, which funded much of Horace's work in Korea.[6] Underwood's rivals in Korea even called him the *millionaire missionary*. (see Fig. 7.8 and 7.9) In fact, missionaries including Underwood at times ventured into trade, importing kerosene, farming implements, and manufactured goods. This suggests that Koreans who were interested in learning about business and capitalism not only found role models in western concessionaries and traders, but also drew familiarity, support, and encouragement from the Protestant clergy.

Fig. 7.9 1901 Underwood Typewriter advertisement. Headquartered in Hartford, Connecticut the manufacturer grew into America's largest producer of typewriters.

Origins of Korean Capitalism

Over the past several decades, the question as to "when" Korean capitalism emerged has frequently surfaced. In the decades that followed World War II, a generation of Korean scholars freed from bindings of Japanese Colonial thought and policy, refuted a viewpoint that Korean capitalism was a product of Japanese rule and progressive thinking. As proof of an earlier proto-industial society, Koreans cited an indigenous market economy that preceded Japanese involvement on the peninsula. Described as the "capitalist sprout school," this model suggests that during the Late Chosôn Dynasty some enterprising Koreans accrued capital from either trade or cash crops, which they used to invest in cottage industries, land, and trade goods. Modeled after successful proto-industrial models, which developed in Japan and China during this period, an ongoing controversy centers on how widespread proto-industrial growth occurred in Korea. To support their argument, Koreans note the rise of labor as a commodity. For example, some nationalists cite that the manufacturing of brassware goods had emerged in P'yôngan and Kyônggi provinces and required a workforce. In addition, wealthy Korean farmers in the rice producing provinces had, too, begun to employ wage earning weaving girls for cottage textile production.[7]

Views do however vary on the origins of Korean capitalism. In the last decade or so, most prominent thinkers have come to agree with conclusions drawn by scholars Carter J. Eckert, Dennis McNamara, and Robert J. Meyers—modern Korean capitalism developed after 1910 and during the Japanese Colonial Period.[8] For example, Koreanist Carter J. Eckert's argument centers on the premise that lacking any substantial commercial or industial development, Korea's social-economic advancements took place during the Japanese Colonial Period. Eckert's work strongly challenges the nationalist Korean historian's proto-industrial "capitalist sprout school" (*chabonjuûi maengaron*).[9] Eckert points out that whatever development did take place it was small in scale, limited by the Korean consumer market, and lacked cohesiveness and interconnectiveness seen in market economies.

Akin to Eckert's work, others experts such as Dennis McNamara argue that the structures and ideas of modern Korean enterprise were non-existent prior to Japanese occupation. He suggests that Korean capitalism is a construct of the political economy of the Chosôn Dynasty, the Colonial experience, and the immediate post-war years. McNamara's work, too, focuses on Japanese Colonial Period entrepreneurs and suggests the experiences of the colonial business elite shaped modern Korean enterprises.

I see the modern economic development of Korea somewhat differently. In fact, in researching this book, my findings suggest that capitalism began to show in the years before the 1905 Japanese Protectorate. To explore this argument further, two factors merit mention. First, the importance of the legal and social changes precipitated by the Kabo reforms and the Sino-Japanese War. Secondly, how popular explanations as to the success of late twentieth century Korean entrepreneurship are equally valid for the first years of the twentieth century before Japanese Colonial rule.

First, the economic landscape of Korea changed considerably in the 1890s. Five centuries of Neo-Confucian mandates that restricted trade and excluded commerce along hereditary and class lines, yielded to progressive Kabo reforms.[10] As noted in earlier sections of this book, reforms begun in 1894 called the *Kabo Kyôngjang* manifested in between 600-to-1,000 new regulations. Paramount among the western-style reforms, *yangban* whose position and livelyhood was once guaranteed by the state faced uncertainty and loss of status. Fortunately, restrictions against the elite's involvement in commerce also were removed. Others, such as the *chungin*, the technocrats, used their language skills and experience interacting with West to enter business.

Subsequently, the Japanese who gained control over the peninsula in the form of a protectorate in 1905 and then intensified with the outright annexation in 1910 repressed this bold generation of fledgling Korean capitalists. Koreans who were involved in the workings of western style commerce, trade, and small business. This generation given time and resources could have expanded their own small businesses and commercial ventures. Unfortunately, it would not be until after the Japanese Colonial Period following World War II that Korean entrepreneurial activities were unrestrained and allowed to soar—a topic discussed at length in the next section of this book.

Modern Thoughts

Management guru Peter Drucker argues that the South Koreans are among the top entrepreneurial people in the world.[11] Drucker notes that the setbacks of the Japanese Colonial Period, the post-World War II split of the country, and Korean War were obstacles to Korea's development; however, Koreans must possess inherent tendencies towards innovation and entrepreneurialism in order to have gained so much in recent decades. Related to this, contemporary western economists find multiple reasons for South Korea's economic success, among these are government policies, a well-educated and disciplined work force, the *dae kiôp* (large-scale business) model, and the relentless drive of the family-run conglomerate founders.[12]

Confucianism's Impact

One other strength recognized by observers today is Korean Neo-Confucian culture—the peninsula's dominate social-political force for over six centuries. Neo-Confucian culture's respect for authority, emphasis on education, loyalty to the family, harmony within the group, and status are often cited as key elements in post-Korean War South Korea's economic rise.[13] I see these characteristics as equally valid in Collbran's time. For example, westerners' early concerns over the ability of Koreans to master modern technology were ill founded. Korean Neo-Confucian emphasis on education meant a ready workforce adept at learning modern technology at both the operational level and management level.[14]

Another Confucian value, loyalty to the family and group, has today as in the past, allowed Koreans to align themselves toward achieving a collective task vital to industrial society and productivity.[15] Together with the Korean Neo-Confucian importance of *inhwa* (harmony), we find a large workforce well suited to tasks requiring cooperation and team-effort.

I propose that the same Neo-Confucian concepts often cited as key factors in the late twentieth century economic success of South Korea were also present prior to the Japanese Colonial rule. Given the late nineteenth century re-structuring of Korean society and the desire for status in the new order, it is not surprising that like today many Koreans quickly created budding businesses—ones that drew upon inherent core Korean Confucian strengths and talents.

Summary

By the end of the nineteenth century, signs of western-style progress were evident in Korea's cities—trains, trolleys, electric lighting, and an occasional automobile. Linked to this progress, capitalism and entrepreneurship was fueled by opportunities for Koreans to enter business, an ever-growing market for goods, and Protestant encouragement. Despite academic arguments that capitalism developed later when Korea fell under Japanese Colonial rule; by the early twentieth century, whether in the rural mountain mining camps of Northern Korea, near the train station in Chemulp'o, or in Seoul's bustling Chongro district, businesses flourished, a viable market economy sprouted, and entrepreneurialism grew.

Fig. 7.10 Chongro district about 1900. In the lower left is the trolley maintenance yard for the Seoul electric trolley system.

Chapter Eight
Lessons Learned

In contrast to the land the first Anglo diplomats, missionaries, and traders had set eyes on in the early 1880s, by the dawn of the twentieth century Korea showed hallmarks of westernization and modernization. Steam-powered locomotives crossed the countryside, ports bustled with commerce, and mining operations carved up the mountainsides. In slightly more than two decades, Seoul too, had transformed. Gone were the days of open sewer drains and scores of bearers hauling water jugs up from the Han River and its tributary streams. Instead a modern waterworks supplied fresh water and a wide boulevard ran between the city's East and West gates. Overhead, like in New York, Chicago, St. Louis, or San Francisco, weaved a maze of telephone, telegraph, and electric power lines. At street-level regular trolley service traversed sections of the city. As Seoul's population grew the city walls and ancient gates could no longer hold the bustle and traffic of trade and commerce. In addition, the once daylong trek by foot from the port of Chemulp'o was reduced to less than two hours by rail and with ten stations enroute before it reached the Seoul Rail Station near the Namdaemun. This meant that by the early twentieth century scores of travelers after departing the train station, grabbed a trolley, and passed en route through the city's ancient gates. Once inside, travelers found Seoul's main thoughfare, Chongro, bustling with activity. In fact, a number of the visitors commented on the city's new look and cleanliness when with compared with other East Asian cites. (see Fig. 8.1)

Fig. 8.1 Seoul main fairway and early commercial district, Chongro, c, 1905

Americans continued to have a highly active role in Korea until 1905. Under agreements with the Japanese government negotiated by President Theodore Roosevelt near the end of the Korea-centered Russo-Japanese War, the United States yielded much of its interest to Japan on the peninsula.[1] As Japanese state-supported business solidified their control of ventures across the peninsula, Americans had an ever-diminishing place in Korea. Some like Dr. Allen and Homer Hulbert returned to United States and lobbied on behalf of Korean self-rule. Others like Hunt and Bostwick moved on to business ventures in the states. A few like the Collbrans stayed until their mines played out. Outside missionary families such as the Underwoods or traders like Walter Townsend, few Americans or their businesses remained in Korea during the Colonial occupation. An interesting exception was the first American-run concession, the Oriental Consolidated Mining Company at Unsan. Amazingly, for nearly forty years the gold mining operation grossed an average of $3,000,000 annually and cumulatively paid out over $14,000,000 in dividends to its English and American backers. Sadly, as was often the case in developing nations, the Korean government since the time of Kojong and then under the Japanese Colonial government only received about $8,500 annually in fees for the "oldest, biggest, richest gold mining company in the Orient".[2] In 1939, the mine nearly played out, was finally sold to a Japanese concern.

Thus, to most Americans with western business interests and investments gone from Korea, it was not until the close of World War Two and under the shadow of the Cold War that Korea came into back into the international spotlight and the focus of the U.S. government.[3] America's crucial role in the Korean War and the subsequent rebuilding of South Korea's economy meant the return of western business involvement on the peninsula. Beginning in the mid 1950s, and growing throughout the 1960s, 1970s, and 1980s a renewed relationship developed between the U.S. and South Korea. In turn, the South Korean economy saw unprecedented double-digit growth for decades—much of its export driven industry supplying cars, electronics, and textiles to American consumers.

History Lessons

Today, glimpses of early U.S.-Korean relations and the *General Sherman* occasionally surface—most often from the Democratic People's Republic of Korea (North Korea). For example, a monument on the banks of the Taedong River in P'yôngyang, the North Korean capital, commemorates the actions taken by its people in 1866 against the foreign invaders. (see Fig. 8.2) Quite revealing of the ongoing contempt for the United States, the monument overlooks the dock where the captured U.S. Naval ship *Pueblo* was moored as a floating museum and North Korean tourist attraction. The contemporary stone pillar is not unlike the 1871 *ch'ôkhwapi* (stone pillars) the Taewon'gun erected across the East Asian peninsula when, too, government policy mandated isolationism and rejected western thought and influence.

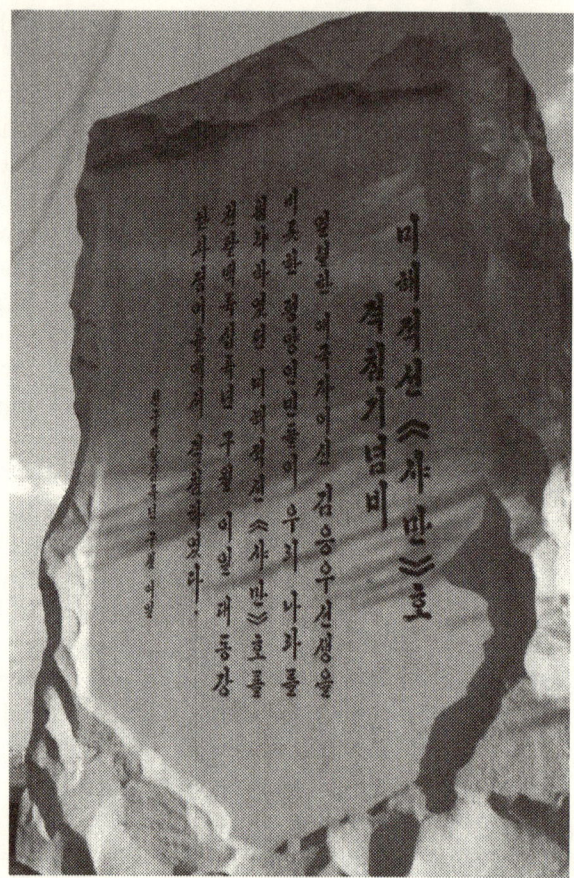

Fig. 8.2 Contemporary monument on the banks of the Taedong (River) near the site of *General Sherman* incident of 1866.

The monument was dedicated in 1986 and states the role of peasant-nationalist Kim Ung Woo (North Korean leader, Kim Il Sung's great grandfather) in leading the military-civilian crowd in repelling the "American pirate ship, the *General Sherman*."

The *General Sherman* and Western Intrusion in North Korean Popular Thought

Even today the *General Sherman* incident finds its way into contemporary North Korean news articles such as "Why Bush Should Study History." These articles cite the *General Sherman* incident as an example of American imperialistic aggression against the peninsula.[4] In turn, one finds North Korean revisionist history linking the current regime's battle with the West as a long-standing family tradition. These histories claim that North Korean president Kim Il Sung's great grandfather Kim Ung Woo led the military-civilian crowd against the *Sherman*.[5] Moreover, Kim Il Sung wrote in his memoirs that his great grandfather settled near P'yôngyang in 1860 and was employed as a caretaker for a wealthy landowner's ancestral burial grounds. The North Korean leader pointed out that although his great grandfather was only a caretaker he was nevertheless an ardent nationalist. When word of the *General Sherman* reached Kim Ung Woo's village and that the ship's crew had killed Koreans, looted the countryside, and kidnapped women, the ancestor joined villagers who gathered up straw ropes and strung them up across the Taedong to block the escape path of the American invaders. Kim Il Sung noted that his great grandfather then boldly led the villagers to P'yôngyang and joined with soldiers and volunteers from other towns, all of whom joined in the final assault of the ship.

Historically, there is no credible evidence Kim Il Sung's ancestor, Kim Ung Woo, ever participated in the attack. In fact, Hwang Jang Yop, a former high ranking official of the North Korean Workers Party who defected to South Korea in 1997, speculated that the ancestor was only about ten years old in 1866.[6] In other words, the *Sherman* incident and its connection to the Kim family appears to be an appropriation of history to support the regime's immediate political goals.[7]

Business Lessons

From Henry Collbran's electric trolley line to his mining projects not to mention other early American business ventures in Korea, we have learned that these enterprises provided training opportunities for legions of quick-learning Koreans who found work as machinists, electricians, railway builders, engineers, and technicians. Other Koreans also tended the western firm's books and served in administrative managerial positions for the construction and operation of public works projects, railways, and mines. This indigenous population learned modern business skills prior to the Japanese Colonial Period. Enterprising Koreans stepped forward during the Enlightenment Era acquired capital and began manu-facturing goods. [See Appendix C] This included entrepreneurs An Hyông Su who established the Daehan Weaving Company, Min Pông Suk who formed the Chongro Weaving Company, and Kim Duk Chang who operated a notable weaving shop.[8] In addition to the textile industry, factories also began to produce ceramics, while others processed tobacco and grains.[9] By 1896, Kim Chong Han, working with other domestic investors, established Chosun Bank, Korea's first modern bank. Soon after, in 1898, Pak Chong Ki founded the Puha Railroad Company. Remarkably, Pak used his own capital to build and run a 3.7-mile rail line between Hatsan and Pusan in Southern Korea. Even in the shadow of the Japanese Protectorate domination, Koreans such as successful merchant Pak Sûng Ik (Park Seung Jik) continued to launch business ventures, specifically the lucra-tive textile and cloth market near the Tongdaemun (Great East Gate). Today, the Tongdaemun market district consists of over thirty shopping centers and about 30,000 stores. In addition, more than 50,000 manufacturing companies join together to trade textiles, clothes, shoes, sports goods, stationery, toys, household goods, and accessories.

In spite of these early business successes and emergence of a budding middle class in South Korea, the Japanese economic-political tactics of the Protectorate years (1905–1909) were such that even seasoned American businessmen such as Collbran and Hunt found the business climate increasingly restrictive and even-tually intolerable. The roots of Korean commerce that developed soon withered under rigid Colonial policy. Hidden for decades it lay dormant. Fortunately, these latent talents would once again emerge and manifest in the 1960s, 1970s, and 1980s in what is frequently described as the economic "Miracle on the Han."

Some Final Words

This work in its early chapters has looked at the barriers to Korean trade with the West. Later chapters found the gradual opening of Korea to foreign trade, west-ern thought, and modernization. The book concludes by witnessing the rise of Korean capitalism and entrepreneurialism. This study has also linked the efforts of American missionaries, traders, and businessmen to western style progress in Korea. Without taking credit away from the sacrifice, discipline, and hard work of the modern Koreans, what stands out by looking back on the accomplishments of the late 1890s and early years of the 1900s was that capitalism and business had firmly taken root on the peninsula. This work strongly suggests that despite centuries of rigid Neo-Confucian thought and norm, the western market model gained support among many Koreans, nurtured by the West, yet the seeds of opportunity had fallen on exceptionally fertile ground. One then cannot dismiss the idea that to better understand today's success the past has much to offer. Hopefully this work will further an understanding of early U.S.-Korean business interactions, while providing valuable insights that link the past to modern Korean business development, entrepreneurialism, and American involvement on the peninsula.

Fig. 8.3 Modern Seoul and Namdaemun (Sungnyemun). The Great South Gate still remains as one of the nation's most treasured landmarks.

Appendix A

Appendix A offers brief biographic sketches on key Anglos discussed in the text.

Notable Anglos

Horace Newton Allen, M.D. (1852–1932) American Protestant missionary-physician turned U.S. diplomat assigned to Korea. Although quarrelsome at times with fellow missionaries in Korea and the State Department in Washington, D.C., he strongly supported American business ventures on the peninsula. Dr. Allen took an increasingly pro-Korea, anti-Japanese posture in the days prior to the establishment of the 1905 Japanese Protectorate, at which time the U.S. legation was disbanded and Allen subsequently returned to America.

John Baptiste Bernadou (1858–1908) In 1884, Smithsonian Institute Secretary Spencer Baird appointed J. B. Bernadou, a recent Naval Academy graduate and newly commissioned naval officer, to gather a collection of material culture from Korea. Interestingly, Baird gave Bernadou the official title of "Smithsonian Attaché" to the American Legation in Seoul. While assigned to this post, the young ensign was asked to investigate the details surrounding the *General Sherman* incident, which had transpired eighteen years earlier. After his assignment in Korea, Bernadou remained active in the military and received a citation for bravery under enemy fire during the Spanish American War.

Harry Rice Bostwick (1870–1931) Junior partner in Seoul-based Collbran and Bostwick Development Company. Bostwick traveled to Korea from San Francisco in the late 1890s to assist in Henry Collbran's growing business endeavors. The partners drew favor from the Korean court with help from Horace Allen to gain the lucrative electric, telephone, water, and streetcar concessions. Following mounting Japanese control over Korea and subsequent sales of the municipal businesses, Bostwick returned to San Francisco in the wake of the earthquake and fire of 1906. He quickly became a land and property developer. In the years that followed, Bostwick frequented Asia on business ventures, as well as, serve as a director of well-known Jesse-Moore Hunt Company and the Bank of Mill Valley, California. His obituary in the *New York Times* noted Bostwick's numerous business accomplishments and official decorations by both the Emperor of Korea and by the Emperor of Japan.

Henry A. Burgevine (1836–1865) American born merchant sailor and self-styled soldier of fortune, Burgevine was recruited in Shanghai as an officer in the "Ever Victorious Army" which fought in the mid-nineteenth century Chinese Taiping War. In 1865, the British Navy captured Burgevine and his rebel crew of mercenaries. His ship, the *General Sherman,* was sold to American merchant W. B. Preston. Soon after, the incarcerated Burgevine mysteriously drowned, while in the custody of Shanghai officials.

Henry Collbran (1852–1925) British-born American entrepreneur, Henry Collbran's early career with railroads led him to Colorado in 1888 as General Manager of the Colorado Midland Railroad. He, then, oversaw numerous railroad construction projects in Colorado serving as Vice-President and Treasurer for the Colorado Midland RR, before becoming President of the Denver-based Midland Terminal RR. A downturn in the mining boom in Colorado prompted Collbran to seek new opportunity in Korea in 1896. Subsequently, he oversaw construction of the first rail line in Korea before obtaining lucrative concessions for the Seoul streetcar, electric, telephone, and water systems. Following the sale of his municipal interests, Collbran focused on mining before retiring to his native London, where he died in 1925 at age 72.

James Scarth Gale (1863–1937) Canadian Presbyterian minister who served in Korea from 1884–1927. Known for his scholastic endeavors, which included an English-Korean dictionary (1897), numerous articles on Korean culture, translations of English texts into Korean, and *The History of the Korean People* (1927).

Leigh Smith John Hunt (1855–1933) Reared in Indiana, Hunt studied and passed the state law bar. He then served in the public school system before becoming president in 1885 of Iowa State Agricultural College (Iowa State University). Soon after, Hunt moved to Seattle and became a newspaper publisher, real estate developer, and president of a local bank. Financial downturns and subsequent bankruptcy led Hunt to Korea to recoup his fortune. First, partnered with James R. Morse, the Seattle businessman soon gained sole control over the hugely profitable Oriental Consolidated Mining Company. So profitable was the mining concession, that by 1901 Hunt was able to repay his Seattle creditors. Like other

American entrepreneurs, ever increasing pressure exerted by Japanese colonialization in Korea led Hunt to leave Korea for new business opportunities elseware. Hunt pursued projects including cotton growing in the Sudan and land development, mining, and agriculture in Las Vegas, Nevada.

James R. Morse Morse, an American expatriate served as longtime president for the American Trading Company of New York and Yokomama, Japan. In 1896, benefiting from the effort of Horace Allen, Morse gained control over the rights to gold production for over 500 square miles in what is today part of North Korea. When concerns over the feasibility of economic mining in Korea grew, Morse sold his interest to Leigh Hunt. Morse whose original interest in Korea had actually been a railroad concession, once again profited from the efforts of Dr. Allen who secured the concession for the nation's first railway from Chemulp'o (Inch'ôn) to Seoul, a twenty-five mile stretch. Morse, not wishing to anger the Japanese who also sought the concession and were an important aspect of his trading business, sold the railroad shortly before it was completed. Over the next few decades, Morse's American Trading Company grew into a global concern with support from financiers including J.P. Morgan.

W. B. Preston (d. 1866) Boston merchant with trading interests in China, Preston obtained the British-seized rebellion ship of Henry Burgevine, the *General Sherman*, in mid-1866. Preston, like his shipmates, died when commoners and soldiers from the P'yôngan region assaulted the *General Sherman*.

Robert. W. Shufeldt (1822–1895) Career naval officer and diplomat, Shufeldt led the initial U.S. investigation into the plight of the *General Sherman*. Years later Commodore Shufeldt returned to the region mandated by the U.S. government to broker a treaty with Korea. The Treaty of Amity and Commerce signed in 1882 gave America extraterritorial rights, low tariffs, and the right for a legation. In turn, the U.S. recognized Korean sovereignty, separate from China.

Robert Jermain Thomas, *Ch'oe Nanhôn* (1839–1866) Welsh-born Protestant missionary assigned to Shanghai by the National Bible Society of Scotland. Upon hearing word of Korean persecution of Christians, the young missionary vowed to bring the word of God to the peninsula. Subsequently, the zealot joined the *Sherman* crew in August 1866, and likewise suffered the fate that befell his comrades. In the decades that followed, Protestants memorialized Thomas' early attempts to spread Christianity on the East Asian peninsula.

Walter Davis Townsend (1856–1918) Boston-born Yankee merchant, Townsend ventured to Japan in the late 1870s and was employed by James R. Morse and the American Clock and Brass Company, a trading company. With the opening of Korea to Americans, Townsend first traveled to Korea in 1884 before taking up lifelong residence on the peninsula, two years later. The Yankee trader's business, initially operating as Morse, Townsend, and Company and was later renamed as Townsend and Co. The firm exported rice to Korea, while importing a wide variety of goods including millions of gallons of kerosene on behalf of the Standard Oil Company. Unlike many of the American missionaries and businessmen, Townsend appears to have maintained a cordial relationship with the Japanese, which meant his business enterprises and assets in Korea saw little attrition under Colonial rule.

Horace Grant Underwood, *Won Du-woo* **(1859–1916)** Vanguard American Presbyterian missionary arrived in Korea in 1885. Soon after, he married fellow missionary Lillias Horton, a woman physician assigned to Korea. Horace was responsible for founding a number of Christian-related organizations including Yonsei University. Following Horace Grant's death, Underwood's wife, their only son Horace Horton Underwood, and subsequently, his prodigy, served for decades as well respected educators in Korea.

Appendix B

Appendix B offers brief biographic sketches on Asians discussed in the text. Asian names are presented in a surname first format and with McCune-Reischauer romanization.

Notable Asians

Chao Ling feng (d. 1866) Chinese crewman on the *General Sherman*. Chao Ling feng, served as interpreter for the *Sherman*'s Anglo leadership. By some accounts, when the ship was under final siege, Chao was one of few to have swam to shore, where he and missionary Robert Thomas were subsequently put to death.

Chông Hôijo Jason Scarth Gale, the Canadian missionary and historian, documented the first-hand account by an "old time hermit" Chông Hôijo, a witness to the incident. Gale's research appeared in the *Korean Repository* in 1895 and in his book, *A History of the Korean People*.

Kim Ung Woo (b. 1856) North Korean leader Kim Il Sung's great grandfather, Kim Ung Woo is reputed to have led the military-civilian crowd against the *Sherman*. Kim Il Sung wrote that his great grandfather settled in Mangyong-dae near P'yôngyang in 1860 and was employed as a caretaker for a landowner Lee Pyong Taek's ancestral burial ground. Kim pointed out that although his great grandfather was only a caretaker he was nevertheless an ardent nationalist. When word of the *General Sherman* reached Kim Ung Woo's village and that the ship's crew had killed Koreans, looted the countryside, and kidnapped women, he joined villagers who gathered up straw ropes and strung them up across the Taedong River to block the escape path of the American invaders. Kim wrote that his ancestor then led his villagers to the P'yôngyang fort and joined with soldiers and volunteers from other towns, all of who joined in the final successful assault of the foreigner's ship.

Kojong, Yi Myôngbok (1852–1919, r. 1864–1907) Ascended to the Korean throne in 1864 when King Ch'ôlchong died sonless. Kojong's father ruled as regent until 1873. The monarch's rule was at a time Korea opened to the West and locked in a struggle to maintain its independence amid the imperialism struggle between Russia, Japan, and China. Kojong sought to gradually modernize his country by introducing western technology and thought to the peninsula. Following the Russo-Japanese War (1904–1905), the Japanese moved to tighten their economic and political grip on the peninsula forming a Protectorate essentially giving them full control. By 1907, Kojong was forced to abdicate as the western world supported Japanese hegemony.

Lee Hyon Ik The deputy commander of P'yôngyang during the 1866 *General Sherman* incident. Lee Hyon Ik acting under orders from P'yôngan Governor Pak Kyusu informed the *Sherman* crew that the King was to be informed of the foreigners' actions—having ignored orders to stay put downriver, pressed on upstream, and insisting on trading—all of which were strictly forbidden. Later after the vessel had neared P'yôngyang, Lee was captured and held hostage by the Anglos before being rescued by Korean soldiers.

Taewon'gun, Yi Hûngson (1820–1898) Born of lesser status within the ruling Yi family, with his son's appointment as king in 1864, Yi Hûngson assumed the title Hûngson Taewon'gun (prince-regent). A distinguished painter and calligrapher, the Taewon'gun was a cunning politician and reformer. Although several of his family were Christians, the Taewon'gun persecuted and massacred thousands of Korean Catholics. His later years were filled with power struggles and plots to overthrow his son, King Kojong.

Pak Kyusu (1807–1877) Grandson of *sirhak* (practical learning) scholar Pak Chiwôn, Pak Kyusu served as P'yôngan provincial governor during the *General Sherman* incident of 1866. Following numerous attempts to turn the Anglo ship back, Pak under direct orders from the Taewon'gun ordered his men assault the *Sherman*. Ironically, Pak became a frequent traveler to China and embraced western learning, technology, and trade.

Pak Ch'ôngwun. Korean drill sergeant who was in charge of the assault on the *General Sherman* in 1866. After freeing Deputy Commander Lee Hyon Ik, Pak mounted a *kôbuksôn* (commonly called a Turtle boat) assault on the *Sherman*. When this failed the Korean sergeant succeeded in setting the *Sherman* afire, overran, and then massacred the crew. Pak for his heroism received praise and promotion to a prestigious military position in the region.

Appendix C

Appendix C offers brief biographic sketches on Korean entrepreneurs discussed in the text. Asian names are presented in a surname first format and with McCune-Reischauer romanization.

Korean Entrepreneurs

An Hyông Su (An Kyongsu) **(1853–1900)** Government finance officer who boldly supported modern business development. As an early Korean entrepreneur, An Hyông Su established the Bank of Chosôn in 1896 and the Daehan Weaving Company (also called the Taehan Textile Mill) in 1897.

Kim Duk Chang Enlightenment Era businessman, Kim Duk Chang formed a weaving company in 1902, which in contrast to other shop owners made use of western textile machines and technology. Prior to his entry into the business sector, Kim served as a high-ranking Chosôn official.

Kim Chong Han (1844–1932) Worked with other domestic investors including An Hyông Su to establish in 1896, the Bank of Chosôn, Korea's first modern bank. Several years later, in 1899, Kim formed a rail transportation service and then continued to be active in the Korean business community for more than a decade.

Min Pông Suk (1858–1940) Korean businessman who formed Seoul's Chongro Weaving Company in 1899. Like many of his peers, Min had once served as a government offical.
Min's other business endeavors included banking and insurance.

Pak Chong Ki (1839–1907) Pioneer in Korean rail development. Pak founded the Puha Railroad Company in 1898. Of interest, Pak used his own capital to build and run a 3.7-mile rail line between Hatsan and Pusan. One of the first Koreans to visit Japan in the 1870s and study its modernization, Pak thereafter devoted his life's mission to modernize Korea.

Pak Sûng Ik (Park Seung jik) Noted Korean merchant who in 1896 opened his first shop in the Paeogae District of Seoul. By 1905, Pak opened a market near the *Tongdaemun* (Great East Gate), which over the years grew into a major textile and trade market. One of the entrepreneur's popular cosmetic products was Pak's Face Powder, which sold for fifty *chôn* (or, one-half *Won,* and was the equivalent to about eight pounds of rice and a day's wage for a skilled worker). Pak's product and life in the market are immortalized in the Korean poem *Mokdye Changt'o.*

Appendix D

Timeline of Key Events in Korea's Past

2333 B.C.	*Tan'gun* mythical founding of Korea.
57 BC–688 AD	Three Kingdom Period (Koguryô, Silla, Paekche, Kaya).
668–918	United Silla Dynasty
918–1392	Koryô Dynasty
1392–1910	Chosôn Dynasty
1592–1598	Japanese invasions.
1627–1636	Manchu invasions.
1866	*General Sherman* Incident
1871	Kanghwa Island Incident
1873	Taewon'gun abdication of throne to King Kojong.
1876	Japan trade agreement with Korea.
1882	Treaty of Amity and Commerce between U.S. and Korea.
1884	Missionary-doctor Horace Allen arrives in Seoul.
1884	Yankee trader Walter D. Townsend begins trade operations in Korea.
1894–1895	Sino-Japanese War ends Chinese suzerainty over Korea, *Kabo Kyôngjang* herald reforms implemented and, first concession granted to American businessman James R. Morse.
1897–1898	Seoul-Chemulp'o (Inch'ôn) railroad constructed.
1899	Seoul Electric Car (trolley) line established

1904–1905	Russo-Japanese War
1905	Japanese Protectorate formed, Horace Allen and American legation recalled.
1908	Collbran-run Seoul Mining Company operates gold and copper mines in northern Korea.
1910–1945	Japanese Colonial Period
1945	Liberation and occupation of Korea by allied forces (U.S and Soviet Union).
1948	Republic of Korea (South Korea) and Democratic People's Republic of Korea (North Korea) divide peninsula geographically and ideologically.
1950–1953	Korean War
1961–1987	Era of authoritarian military control in South Korea. Period of rapid modernization, urbanization, and industrialization. Rise of Korean big business (dae kiôp).
1987	End of authoritarian controlled government. Free and open democratic elections held in South Korea.
1988	Seoul hosts XXIV Summer Olympic Games.
1997	Asian fiscal crisis rocks South Korean economy.
2004	South Korea ranked among largest global economies.

Appendix E

Korean Geography: Important Places and Cities

Chemulp'o   Port district of the western coastal city of Inch'ôn that through its proximity to Seoul grew in importance during the opening of Korea to the West.

Chongro   (Bell Street) Main thoughfare dating back to old Seoul that ran directionally east-to-west between the *Tongdaemun* (Great East Gate) and the Sôdaemun (Great West Gate). During the Early Modern Era it emerged one of Seoul's first centers of commerce.

Ch'ôlsan   Coastal region in North P'yôngan province.

Hansông   (Fortress of the Han) One of several traditional names for the walled and gated city of Seoul.

Hwanghae   Korean province north of Seoul and south of P'yôngyang.

Kaesông   Korean city of ancient heritage forty miles north of Seoul. During the Late Chosôn Dynasty and Early Modern Era it was a center of trade, manufacturing, and commerce.

Kanghwa Island   (river flower) Rich with history reaching back eons, its strategic location at the mouth of the Han River meant it was often a site of conflict during the nineteenth century.

Kapsan   District in Ryangyang province of North Korea, site of massive Collbran-run copper mining operation.

Kyônggi   (royal domain) Korean province that includes Seoul and Inch'ôn.

Pusan   Port city in Korea's southeast coast. For centuries it served as the main place of trade between Korean and Japanese merchants, for which the later developed inroads and made heavy investments during the late nineteenth century.

P'yôngan   North Korean province, which covers the region near P'yôngyang. North P'yôngan's Yalu River borders China.

P'yôngyang   Korean city of ancient heritage, its significance reaches back to the founding myth of Tan'gun. During the Early Modern Era it emerged as a center of both commerce and Protestantism.

Seoul (Sôul) Ancient Korean city that achieved prominence with its selection as the capital city for the Chosôn Dynasty. The center of Neo-Confucian bureaucratic political control and hegemony, it was also the hub of commercial and economic activity.

Suan   Area located in Hwanghae province about 40 miles southeast of P'yôngyang. Suan was the site of early twentieth century Collbran-run gold mining operations.

Ulsan   Port city on Korea's southeastern coast. By the late twentieth century it grew into the heavy industry hub for much of the Hyundai Group's manufacturing empire.

Unsan   Mining area in North P'yôngan province, site of Leigh Hunt's highly successful concession, the Consolidated Mining Company.

Wonson   Port city on Korea's east coast. With Pusan and Chemulp'o (Inch'ôn) it was one of the first ports opened to Japanese and, soon after, western trade.

Endnotes

Chapter One

[1]   Kyung Moon Hwang, *Beyond Birth: Social Status in the Emergence of Modern Korea* (Cambridge, MA: Harvard University Press, 2004), p. 339.

[2]   This work does not discount the entrepreneurial influence of scores of Chinese and Japanese traders, shop owners, and merchants who traveled to Korea during the late nineteenth century for trade and commerce. Actually, for centuries, Japan and China had been Korea's active trade partners in the region. However, as Korea opened to the West, Chinese and Japanese business sought to capitalize on new opportunities on the East Asian peninsula. No doubt, some Koreans benefited from observing and interacting with the sojourners. With regard to the positive impact of non-Asians, following the trade agreement with the U.S. in 1882, other western nations entered in trade treaties with Korea. As Korea strove to westernize, experts from Prussia (Germany) and then Great Britain were instrumental in the nation adopting modern trade, commerce, and governmental policy. For example, in the early 1880s, Prussian-born Paul-Georg von Möllendorff served for three years as a high ranking and influential custom's administrator. Möllendorff was succeeded by Americans Henry Merrill and Owens Denny, who also made strides to modernize government economic policy. Perhaps, the most successful of the non-Asians working for the Korean government was John McLeavey Brown. Brown, a strong-willed Irishman, served as Chief Financial Advisor to the monarchy beginning in 1893. Nevertheless, notwithstanding the contributions of these westerners, this book centers on the connection of American and Korean business and commercial interaction, especially on Korea's budding capitalistic economy.

[3]   Alfred Marshall, *Principles of Economics* 9th ed. (New York: Macmillan, 1961) in his 1890 work noted entrepreneurs as: the driving force behind industry, act with limited information, and that entrepreneurship was a rare skill. Harvey Leibenstein, in essay 14 of T*he Collected Essays of Harvey Leibenstein*, vol. 2, Kenneth Button, ed. (Aldershot, England: Edward Elgar Publishing, 1989) argues that the dominant characteristic of entrepreneurs is their ability to perceive gaps in markets. They then develop new goods, services, or processes to fit those needs.

Moreover, Leibenstein points out that entrepreneurs have the ability to innovatively combine various inputs to satisfy the market. In addition, Peter Drucker, *Innovation and Entrepreneurship: Practice and Principles* (New York: Harper and Row, 1985) found that in some cases (typically in less developed nations), entrepreneurs may not produce a new product but use creative innovation to apply knowledge and technology developed elseware to their market niche.

⁴   In the post-Korean War recovery period, Syngman Rhee, amid his "March North" slogan, created a U. S. supported free market economy that followed an import substitution industrialization (ISI) model. Rhee sought a self-reliant industrial base (steel, chemicals, machine tools and electrical power) in a market protected from Japanese products. Begrudgingly the U.S. government indulged aspects of Rhee's political economic plan.

⁵   Officially, the United States government had shown little interest in Korea during the pre-Civil War period. The Hermit Kingdom—a name some westerners gave to the foreign land came into common usage after the publication of William Elliot Griffis's, 1882 *Corea, The Hermit Kingdom*, which fueled intrigue in the East Asian nation popularly known for its remoteness and isolationist policy

⁶   This rather lengthy notation highlights interest in the *Sherman* story for more than a century. This first list includes venerable English language versions of the incident: William Elliot Griffis, *Corea, The Hermit Kingdom* (1882; reprint, New York: Charles Scriber's Sons, 1897); John Ross, *History of Korea* (London: Elliot Stock, 1891); Joseph H. Longford, *The Story of Korea* (London: T. Fisher Unwin, 1911); Homer B. Hulbert, *Hulbert's The History of Korea,* vol. 2, ed. Clarence Norwood Weems (New York: Hillary House Publishers Ltd., 1962); F. A. McKenzie, *Korea's Fight for Freedom* (New York: Fleming H. Revell Company, 1920); Charles Oscar Paullin, *Diplomatic Negotiations of American Naval Officers, 1778–1883* (Baltimore, MD: Johns Hopkins Press, 1912); James Scarth Gale, "The Fate of the General Sherman," *The Korean Repository*, vol. 2 (New York: Paragon Book Reprint Corp., 1964); Richard Rutt, *James Scarth Gale and History of the Korean People* (Seoul: Korean Branch of the Royal Asiatic Society, 1972); Oh Moon Whan, "The Two Visits of the Reverend R. J. Thomas to Korea," *Transactions of the Korean Branch of the Royal Asiatic Society* 22 (1933); and E.M. Cable, "United States-Korean Relations, 1866–1871," *Transactions of the Korea Branch of the Royal Asiatic Society* 28 (1938).

The second group are Korean language sources: "제너럴셰만호전," *Han'guk Minjok Munhwa Taebaekkwa Sajon* (Kyonggi-do Songnam-si : Han'guk Chongsin

Munhwa Yon'guwon: Seoul : Konggupch'o Ungjin Ch'ulp'an Chusik Hoesa, 1991); *Kojong Sillok*, Year 3, King Kojong Royal Archives. One final Korean source is the *Kunse Chosôn Chônggam*, where the *General Sherman* incident is discussed within the Han-Kyo Kim translations of Peter Lee, ed., *The Sourcebook of Korean Civilization*, vol. 2 (New York: Columbia University Press, 1996).

Other valuable sources that discuss the event include: Ching Young Choe, *The Rule of the Tae Won' Gun, 1864–1873: Restoration in Yi Korea* (Cambridge, MA: Harvard East Asian Monographs, 1972); Robert T. Oliver, *A History of the Korean People in Modern Times: 1800 to Present* (London and Toronto: Associated University Presses, 1993); Melvin Frederick Nelson, *Korea and the Old Orders in Eastern Asia* (Baton Rouge, LA: Louisiana State University Press, 1945); Washington, U.S. Government. Printing Office, *Papers Relating to the Foreign Relations of the United States, 1861–1928*, 1867, 1868, and 1871.

Chapter Two

¹   Western thought entered Korea in the eighteenth century through the preaching and doctrine of Catholicism. Chai-Sik Chung noted that their own intellectuals, not Western missionaries first introduced Catholicism to Korea. Vigorous debates among the scholar class over the compatibility of the two belief systems led to what Don Baker labeled a "Catholic-Confucian divide"—orthodoxy versus heterodoxy. See Don Baker, "A Different Thread: Orthodoxy, Heterodoxy, and Catholicism in a Confucian World," *Culture and the State in Late Chosôn Korea*, eds. Ja Hyun Kim Haboush and Martina Deuchler (Cambridge, MA: Harvard University Press, 1999), pp. 199–230. See also Chai-Sik Chung, A *Korean Encounter with the Western World* (Berkeley, CA: Institute of East Asian Studies, University of California at Berkeley, 1995), pp. 39–42 and 72–73; and "Tradition and Ideology: Korea's Initial Response to Christianity from a Religious and Sociological Perspective," *Asian Culture* 4 (October 1988): 115–146.

²   Martina Deuchler argued in *The Confucian Transformation of Korea* (Cambridge, MA: Harvard University Press, 1992) that Neo-Confucianism was "the driving force" in the dynamism, which led to the establishment of the Chosôn Dynasty (1392–1910) by intellectuals. Moreover, she stated that Neo-Confucian learning became an ideological tool used by bureaucrats to "reshape the sociopolitical environment" and promote order.

³   Chung, *A Korean Encounter with the Western World*, p. 41.

4   Ki-Baek Lee, *A New History of Korea*, trans. Edward W. Wagner with Edward J. Shultz (Seoul, Korea: Ilchokak Publishers, 1984), pp. 174–175.

5   Hwang, *Beyond Birth: Social Status in the Emergence of Modern Korea*, p. 340.

6   Edward Wagner, Carter Eckert, et al., *Korea: Old and New, A History* (Cambridge, MA: Harvard University Press, 1990), p. 199.

7   Stewart Lone and Gavan McCormick, *Korea: Since 1850* (New York: St. Martin Press, 1993), p. 6.

8   Seoul was a walled and gated city with the Namdaemun serving as the southwestern entrance to the city. Also called the Sungnyemun, the Namdaemun, along with the Tongdaemun (Great East Gate), and the Sôdaemun (Great West Gate) were focal points of commerce and public activity during the Chosôn Dynasty.

9   See James B. Palais, *Politics and the Policy in Traditional Korea* (Cambridge, MA: Harvard University Press, 1975), pp. 24–27, for a detailed explanation of Kojong's succession.

10   M.J. Rhee, *The Doomed Empire: Japan in Colonial Korea* (Brookfield, VT: Ashgate Publishing Company, 1997), p. 6.

11   Bruce Cumings, *Korea's Place in the Sun: A Modern History* (New York: W.W. Norton, 1997), p. 100.

12   Oliver, *A History of the Korean People in Modern Times*, pp. 49–50.

13   Lee Sun-keum insightfully described in "Some Lesser-Known Facts About Taewongun and His Foreign Policy," *Transactions of the Korean Branch of the Royal Asiatic Society* 39 (1962): 23–24, that the Taewon'gun was not blindly opposed to Christianity, but a was reformist and "politician of the highest grade."

14   Gregory Henderson, *The Politics of the Vortex* (Cambridge, MA: Harvard University Press, 1968), pp. 60–61; and Fredrick Foo Chien, *The Opening of Korea: A Study of Chinese Diplomacy, 1876–1885* (Hamden, CT: The Shoe String Press, Inc., 1967), pp. 18–19.

15   Chung, *A Korean Encounter with the Western World*, p. 41.

16   H. Doc., Extension of American Commerce-Proposed Mission to Japan and Corea, 28th Cong., 2nd Sess., 15 February 1845, U.S. Congress, Executive Documents, vol. 3. And, Coleman, *American Images of Korea*, pp. 29–30.

[17] Tyler Dennett, *Americans in Eastern Asia: A Critical Study of United States' Policy in the Far East in the Nineteenth Century* (1922, New York: Barnes & Noble, 1963), pp. 407–421. For a work on Seward's foreign policy see: Ernest N. Paolino, *The Foundations of The American Empire: William Henry Seward and The U.S. Foreign Policy* (Ithaca, NY: Cornell University Press, 1973).

[18] Fred Harvey Harrington, "An American View of Korean-American Relations." *Korean-American Relations, 1866–1997,* eds. Yur-Bok Lee and Wayne Patterson (Albany, NY: State University of New York Press, 1999), pp. 36–37.

[19] See "Depositions by Seamen," U.S. consul in Shanghai (Robert C. Murphy) to William L. Marcy, 22 December 1855, "Dispatches from United States Consuls in Shanghai, 1847–1906," 3 (28 July 1855–31 December 1866), File Microcopies of Records in the National Archives. no. 112, roll 3, National Archives, Washington, D.C. And, Earl Swisher, "The Adventures of Four Americans in Korea and Peking in 1855," *Pacific Historical Review* 21 (August 1952): 237–41 and Swisher's *China's Management of the American Barbarians: A Study of Sino-American Relations, 1841–1861, with Documents* (New York: Octagon Books, 1972), pp. 308–309.

[20] Ching Young Choe, *The Rule of the Tae Won' Gun*, pp. 109–110 and *Foreign Relations*, 1867, Part 1, pp. 414–416.

Chapter Three

[1] William M. Lytle and Forrest R. Holdcamper, *Merchant Steam Vessels of the U.S.: 1790–1868*, ed. C. Bradford Mitchell (Staten Island, NY: The Steamship Historical Society of America, 1975), pp. 82 and 198; And, Erik Heyl, *Early American Steamers*, vol. 1 (Buffalo, NY: 1953).

[2] According to data provided by naval historians William M. Lytle and Forrest R. Holdcamper, I see only two of the three ships, which were named the *General Sherman*, of sufficient displacement. However, only one, number 22,276 (the former Confederate *Princess Royal*) is described as a blockade-runner complete with Civil War era armaments. In addition, Erik Heyl's text, *Early American Steamers*, charts the history of a former *Princess Royal*, one that coincides with our story.

[3] William Speer, "Corea: What Shall We Do," *The Galaxy* 13 (March 1872): 309. Published by Sheldon and Company, New York, 1872.

⁴   See Oh Moon Whan, "The Two Visits of the Reverend R. J. Thomas to Korea," 110–111.

⁵   Spencer J. Palmer, *Korea and Christianity: The Problem of Identification with Tradition* (Seoul: Hollym, Royal Asiatic Society Branch, 1967), pp. 72–73.

⁶   Keith Pratt and Richard Rutt, *Korea: A Historical and Cultural Dictionary* (Surrey, England: Curzon Press, 1999), p. 469.

⁷   The French fleet departed in late September. The expedition was in response to the Taewon'gun's execution of French Catholics priests in 1866.

⁸   Griffis in *Corea: The Hermit Kingdom*, and a later work, *Corea: Without and Within* (Philadelphia, 1885), strongly suggests the crew had a less than noble plan, a view seen in the works of Hulbert, Longford, and McKenzie. Ross, in *History of Korea*, was less critical: "the Europeans were kindly treated for some days; but after news from the capital, they were enticed a shore and put to death, the ship surrounded, and set on fire." p. 294.

⁹   Griffis, *Corea: The Hermit Kingdom* (1897 edition), pp. 391–394.

¹⁰   Ibid., footnote, p. 391–392.

¹¹   See also Longford, *The Story of Korea*, pp. 232–233.

¹²   A consensus among recent works presents the expedition's mission in less favorable terms. See Coleman, *Americans Images of Korea*, p. 33; Claude A. Buss, "At the Beginning," *Reflections on a Century of United States-Korean Relations, Conference Papers, June 1982* (Washington, D.C.: Academy of Korean Studies and The Wilson Center, University Press of America, 1983), p. 46; and Andrew C. Nahm, ed., "American-Korean Relations, 1866–1878, An Overview," *The United States and Korea: American-Korean Relations, 1866–1976* (Kalamazoo, MI: The Center for Korean Studies, 1979), p. 10.

¹³   Harrington, "An American View of Korean-American Relations," p. 37.

¹⁴   In 1637, China and Korea signed a treaty formalizing their religio-philosophical loyalties. China as the "middle kingdom" assumed an elder brother role. This meant both countries' leaders recognized Korea's sovereign right to govern its own domestic matters. Korea's leaders, in turn, were expected to follow China's guidance in external affairs. This complex association was difficult for Western powers to interpret, especially for nations wishing to trade with Korea. Moreover, Korean officials, when to their advantage, used their relationship with China to shield themselves from direct involvement with the West.

[15] Whan, "The Two Visits of the Reverend R. J. Thomas to Korea," 95–123.

[16] Chông Hôijo, in *Gale's The History of The Korean People* suggests that Pak Kyusu sent Colonel Chông Ch'ihyôn to the ship; however, most other sources name Lee Hyon Ik.

[17] Rutt, *James Scarth Gale and History of the Korean People*, p. 311.

[18] McKenzie in *Korea's Fight for Freedom* pointed out the belief among Koreans that dragon cloud armor was impervious to bullets.

[19] See Gordon H. Chang, "Whose 'Barbarism'? Whose 'Treachery'? Race and Civilization in the Unknown United States-Korea War of 1871," *The Journal of American History* 89 (2003): 1349. Chang notes that in the 1871 war, Korean cannons captured by U.S. forces dated from the sixteenth and seventeenth century.

[20] Griffis, *Corea: The Hermit Nation* (1897), pp. 393–394, footnote.

[21] Quote attributed to William M. Baird's article in *The Independent*, 20 May 1897. See Kyung Moon Hwang, "From Dirt to Heaven: Northern Koreans in the Chosôn and Early Modern Eras," *Harvard Journal of Asiatic Studies*, 62 (June 2002): 135–137.

[22] Ibid.

[23] Gale's versions of Lee Hyon Ik's capture tells of the deputy commander being detained on the *General Sherman* and rescued by Pak Ch'ôngwun in a assault on the armed *Sherman*. However, in carefully reviewing Cable's work and the multiple sources he presents, Lee was rescued prior to the successful final attack. For Pak Ch'ôngwun to board the *General Sherman* earlier would have proved a formidable task and meant confronting the bulk of the schooner's crew versus overpowering a beached and lightly armed six-man dingy.

[24] Ibid.

[25] Gale, "The Fate of the General Sherman," pp. 252–254; and Rutt, *James Scarth Gale and History of the Korean People*, pp. 310–311 and 352.

[26] The son of the victim was subsequently raised in Chông's home. See Gale, "The Fate of the General Sherman," pp. 252–254.

[27] Rutt, *Gale's History*, p. 311.

[28]   Griffis, *Corea, The Hermit Kingdom* (1897 version), p. 395. Bernadou traveled from Seoul to P'yôngyang in 1884 (eighteen years after the incident) to conduct the investigation.

[29]   Cable, "United States-Korean Relations, 1866–1871," 25.

[30]   Gale pointed out in his 1895 *Korean Repository* article, some twenty-nine years after the *Sherman incident*, that the cannons and chain were still on display.

[31]   Cable derived much of his work from the *Kojong Sillok*, Chapter XXII, Report VIII, "The Report on the Destruction of the Foreign Vessel," dated July 27, 1866 (lunar calendar) or Saturday September 6, 1866 (Western calendar).

[32]   The *General Sherman's* resurrection appeared in an article by Kyutae Rhee, a senior reporter for *Chosun Ilbo*. For a Korean version of the story, see: NK Chosun.com October 30, 2002 online edition. Moreover, Pak Chehyôn (1845–1884) in the *Kunse Chosôn Chônggam* stated that the *Sherman* upon seizure was moved near Seoul on the Han River, dismantled and rebuilt at considerable costs. See Han-Kyo Kim's translation in Lee, *The Sourcebook of Korean Civilization*, pp. 309–310. Pak Chehyôn's account of the *Sherman* incident presents a version on the fate of the ship different from the government "official" story. The *Kunse Chosôn Chônggam* (despite some factual inaccuracies) provides eyewitness accounts of key court events and policies

Chapter Four

[1]   *Foreign Relations*, 1867, Part 1, p. 427.

[2]   Key-Huik Kim, *The Last Phase of the East Asian World Order: Korea, Japan, and the Chinese Empire, 1860–1882* (Berkeley, CA: University of California Press, 1980), pp. 52–53 and *Foreign Relations*, 1867, Part 1, p. 416.

[3]   Ibid.

[4]   Ibid. For the dynamics of Japanese involvement in the aborted *bakufu* intervention in Korea see Key-Hiuk Kim's work on pp. 101–109.

[5]   Dennett, *Americans in Eastern Asia*, pp. 418–420.

[6]   *Foreign Relations*, 1867, Part. I, p. 426.

[7]   See Frederick C. Drake, *The Empire of the Seas: A Biography of Rear Admiral Robert Wilson Shufeldt, USN* (Honolulu, HI: University of Hawaii Press, 1984),

pp. 101–103. Drake's work describes, in detail, Shufeldt's investigation into the *Sherman* incident.

[8] Washington, D.C.: Government Printing Office, 1867. Gideon Welles, Secretary of the Navy, 1867.

[9] Drake, *The Empire of the Seas*, p. 102.

[bp] See Lytle, *Merchant Steam Vessels of the U.S.: 1790–1868*, p.198; and, Heyl, *Early American Steamers*.

[11] Ibid.

[12] *Foreign Relations*, 1868, Part 1, pp. 554–547. S. Wells Williams, U.S. Chargé d' Affaires ad interim noted meeting with one of the Korean mission's members confidentially and obtained the particulars of the attack. Perhaps, Wells in these closed door meetings negotiated for the discreet return of the ship with the Korean mission.

[13] See Gordon H. Chang's scholarship on the 1871 expedition. Chang's article provides a comprehensive study on the war. Chang, "Whose 'Barbarism'? Whose 'Treachery'? Race and Civilization in the Unknown United States-Korea War of 1871," 1331–1365.

Chapter Five

[1] John Y. Simon, ed. *The Papers of Ulysses S. Grant*, vol. 22, June 1, 1871–January 31, 1872 (Carbondale, IL: Southern Illinois University Press, 1998), p. 271.

[2] Ibid.

[3] Chung, A *Korean Encounter with the Western World*, pp. 40–41. Quote from *Kojong Sillok* in *Kojong Sunjong Sillok*, reprint of the edition owned by Han'guk Kyohoe yôn'guso, 3 vols. plus index vol. (Seoul: T'amguadang, 1970), 3:43b; see also 3:82b–83a.

[4] Two excellent works of western scholarship on the concept of *sei-Kan* (conquer Korea) include Hilary Conroy, *The Japanese Seizure of Korea: 1868–1910, The Study of Realism and Idealism in International Relations* (Philadelphia, PA: University of Pennsylvania Press, 1960) and Peter Duus, *The Abacus and the Sword: The Japanese Penetration of Korea, 1895–1910* (Berkeley, CA: University of California Press, 1995).

5   Chung, A *Korean Encounter with the Western World*, pp. 72–73. Palais, *Politics and Policy*, pp. 176–201.

6   Martina Deuchler, *Confucian Gentlemen and Barbarian Envoys: The Opening of Korea, 1875–1885* (Seattle, WI: University of Washington, 1977), p. 14.

7   Li Hongzhang, was a protégé of Empress Dowager Tz'u-hsi who although not the emperor actually ruled China. From 1870–1895, Li held many concurrent positions including grand secretary, governor-general of Zhili province, and high commissioner for the Northern Ocean.

8   Wagner, *Korea: Old and New, A History*, p. 199.

9   Ibid.

10   The order came for Secretary of State James Blaine. Blaine, a Yankee from Maine, was influenced by a maritime constituency to promote trade in the Pacific. Furthermore, domestic economic panics of the 1870s forced American manufacturers to look for foreign markets, a cause heralded by Blaine. See Edward P. Crapol, *James G. Blaine: Architect of Empire* (Wilmington, DE: SR Books, 2000). Drake's *The Empire of the Seas*, Chapter 12, describes Shufeldt's at times challenging quest to craft the trade treaty with Korea.

11   Deuchler, *Confucian Gentlemen and Barbarian Envoy*, p. 114.

12   See Robert R. Swartout, Jr., *Mandarins, Gunboats, and Power Politics: Owen Nickerson Denny and the International Rivalries in Korea* (Honolulu, HI: University Press of Hawaii, 1980).

13   McCune, *Korean-American Relations*, pp. 44–45.

14   Ibid.

15   Ibid.

16   Ibid.

Chapter Six

1   Allen was not alone in building influence with the monarchy. In 1886, American Owen Nickerson Denny had been appointed a position within the Korean government. Denny, too, strove to develop Korea economically and saw potential in the country's natural resources, especially in the P'yôngan province. See Swartout, *Mandarin, Gunboats, and Power*, p. 129.

2   Harrington, "An American View of Korean-American Relations, p. 37.

3   D.L. Mundy, *God and Rich Society: A Study of Christians in a World of Abundance* (New York: Oxford Press, 1961), p. 26.

4   Max Weber, *The Protestant Ethic and the Spirit of Capitalism*, Talcott Parsons, trans. (New York: Routledge, 2002), p. xiii. For a survey on Weber's work regarding capitalism see also Gianfranco Poggi, *Calvinism and the Capitalist Spirit: Max Weber's Protestant Ethic* (Amherst, MA: University Of Massachusetts Press, 1983), pp. 13–39.

5   Robert Wauzzinski, *Between God and Gold; Protestant Evangelicalism and the Industrial Revolution, 1820–1914* (Rutherford, NJ: Fairleigh Dickenson University Press, 1993), p. 63.

6   Ibid., p. 91.

7   See Harold F. Cook, *Pioneer American Businessman in Korea; The Life and Times of Walter Davis Townsend* (Seoul: Royal Asiatic Society, Korea Branch, 1981).

8   Ibid., pp. 13–14.

9   Lilias Horton Underwood, *Fifteen Years Among the Top-Knots* (Seoul: Royal Asiatic Society, Korea Branch Kyung-In Publishing Co., 1977), p. 4.

10   McKenzie, *Korea's Fight for Freedom*, p. 23.

11   Homer Hulbert, *Hulbert's History of Korea*, p. 284. See also Wagner, *Korea: Old and New, A History*, pp. 224–225.

12   Horace N. Allen, *Things Korean: A Collection of Sketches and Anecdotes Missionary and Diplomatic* (New York: Fleming H. Revell Company, 1908), p. 232. For a fascinating study on Allen's work in Korea see Fred Harvey Harrington, *God, Mammon, and the Japanese: Dr. Horace Allen and Korean-American Relations, 1884–1905* (Madison, WI: University of Wisconsin Press, 1944). Another often cited source is the Allen Manuscripts in the New York Public Library.

13   William Franklin Sands, *Undiplomatic Memories: The Far East 1896–1904* (New York: Whittlesey House, 1930), pp. 197–198. See also Lee, *A New History of Korea*, p. 301 for a chart on Korean concessions granted 1883–1898.

14   Donald N. Clark, *Living Dangerously in Korea: The Western Experience 1900–1950* (Norwalk, CT: EastBridge Press, 2003), Chapter 11, pp. 222–239 gives an in depth study of the Oriental Consolidated Mining Company.

[15] Edwin W. Mills, "Gold Mining in Korea," *The Korean Branch of the Royal Asiatic Society* 7 (1916): 23–24.

[16] Spencer J. Palmer, "American Gold Mining in Korea's Unsan District," *Pacific Historical Review* 31 (1962): 381.

[17] Dean Alexander Arnold, *American Economic Enterprises in Korea, 1895–1939* (New York: Arno Press, 1976), pp. 56–57.

[18] Ibid., p. 65. And, Dean Alexander Arnold, "Collbran of Colorado: Concessionaire in Korea," *Colorado Quarterly* (Summer 1959): 7.

[19] J.S. Collbran, "Notes on Henry Collbran," Henry Collbran Papers, Colorado State Historical Society, (hereafter called the Collbran Papers) MSS 128. Box 2, FF# 12. p. 1a.

[20] Arnold, *American Economic Enterprises in Korea*, p. 73.

[21] Palmer, "American Gold Mining in Korea's Unsan District," 382–383.

[22] Allen, *Things Koreans*, pp. 233–234.

[23] Sands, *Undiplomatic Memories*, p. 203.

[24] Ada E. Leeke and Evelyn Shaw, *When American Came to Korea* (Freeman, SD: Pine Hill Press, 1991), p. 167.

[25] *Tongnip Sinmun (The Independent)*, September 1899.

[26] Horace G. Underwood, *The Call of Korea: Political-Social-Religious* (New York: Fleming H. Revell Company, 1908), p. 24.

[27] Leeke, *When American Came to Korea*, p. 168.

[28] John S. Collbran and Eleanor C. Merrick, "Notes on a Conversation between John S. Collbran and Eleanor C. Merrick on November 26, 1969 Concerning the Collbran Family History," Collbran Papers, MSS 128, Box 2, FF# 17, p. 2.

[29] Yi Kyu-tae, *Modern Transformation of Korea*, trans. Sung Tong-mahn, Charles Goldberg, et al., (Seoul: Sejong Publishing Company, 1970), p. 300.

[30] Ibid., p. 310. Interestingly, the early Korean streetcars are similar in design to that of the present day San Francisco "California" style cable cars, although the later operate by on a cable system and not electricity. Nevertheless, the car's seating layout and configuration appear to be the same.

31 Hulbert, *Hulbert's History of Korea*, pp. 277–278.

32 Another reason that Collbran offered films to the public was to offset the negative publicity of several accidental trolley deaths.

33 J.S. Collbran, "Notes on Henry Collbran," Collbran Papers, MSS 128. Box 2, FF # 12, p. 2.

34 Arnold, "Collbran of Colorado," 11.

35 William Franklin Sands (1874–1946). In 1900, Sands, the former secretary of the American legation in Seoul, became advisor to the Emperor Kojong, a post he maintained until 1904. A friend of Collbran and Bostwick, Sands' views most often were pro-Korean.

36 Americans called the company the American Korean Electric Company, Korean sources reverse the names.

37 Mills, "Gold Mining in Korea," 24.

38 Beginning in 1907, Harry Bostwick's name appeared in the San Francisco business directories and was listed as a "capitalist." In 1908 and 1909, Harry along with brother Frank were also listed as partners in the real estate firm, Barker, Knickerbocker, and Bostwick. Ashbrook Lincoln, "San Francisco Bay-Area Views of Russian Aggression in Far East, 1903–1905," *California Historical Society Quarterly* 30 (1951): 205.

39 Clark, *Living Dangerously in Korea*, p. 228 footnote.

40 Ibid., p. 230.

Chapter Seven

1 Arnold, *American Economic Enterprises in Korea*, p. 73.

2 Howard H. Stevenson, Michael J. Roberts, et al., *New Business Ventures and the Entrepreneur* (Boston, MA: Irwin McGraw-Hill, 1999), p. 1.

3 Kyeyong Park, *The Korean American Dream: Immigrants and Small Business in New York City* (Ithaca, NY: Cornell University Press, 1997). Park notes that Korean immigrants to America employed old ideologies and a propensity to establish small businesses as a route to the American dream.

[4]   Dae Young Ryu, "Understanding Early American Missionaries In Korea (1884–1910); Capitalist Middle-Class Values and the Weber Thesis," *Archives de Sciences Sociales des Religions* 113 (Javier-Mars) 2001: 93–118.

[5]   Ibid., p. 91.

[6]   Clark, *Living Dangerously in Korea,* p. 14.

[7]   Lone, *Korea, Since 1850,* p. 6.

[8]   Carter J. Eckert, *Offspring of Empire: The Koch'ang Kims and the Colonial Origins of Korean Capitalism, 1876–1945* (Seattle, WA: University of Washington, 1991), Dennis L. McNamara, *The Colonial Origins of Korean Enterprise, 1910–1945* (New York: Cambridge University Press, 1990), p. x, 1–5. Robert J. Myers, *Korea in the Cross Currents: A Century of Struggle and the Crisis of Reunification* (New York: Palgrave, 2001), pp. 31–32.

[9]   Park Chan-Seung, "Should Korean Historians Abandon Nationalism?" *Korea Journal,* (Summer 1999): 322.

[10]   Deuchler, *Confucian Gentlemen and Barbarian Envoy,* p. 127.

[11]   George Gendron, "Flashes of Genius," *Inc. Magazine* (May 1996). An interview with Peter Drucker on entrepreneurial complacency.

[12]   Kae H. Chung, "An Overview of Korean Management," *Korean Managerial Dynamics,* eds. Kae H. Chung and Hak Chong Lee (New York: Praeger, 1989), p. 3. In addition and within the book, see Shim and Steers, "The Entrepreneurial Basis of Korean Enterprise: Past Accomplishments and Future Challenges," p. 25 where the authors note that the Republic of Korea's economic success must include recognizing the national commitment by the masses to build a better nation.

As for the name western scholarship and journalism most often labels the family-run conglomerates—*chaebol* (literally, financial cliques)—in South Korea the term has taken on a derogatory association with the financial crisis of 1997. A more acceptable term is perhaps *dae kiôp.*

[13]   Chung, "An Overview of Korean Management," pp. 4–5.

[14]   Ibid.

[15]   Ibid.

Chapter Eight

[1] Japanese control was essentially unchallenged after July of 1905 with the Taft-Katsura Memorandum. Then, under the terms of the Treaty of Portsmouth, which ended the Russo-Japanese War (1904–1905), Japan was granted paramount military, political, and economic control over the peninsula. Roosevelt felt the Japanese were best prepared to modernize their Asian neighbor. Nevertheless, Roosevelt wanted an open door policy that still protected U.S. interest on the peninsula including the American mining concessions granted under Kojong.

[2] "Choson Gold," *Time Magazine* September 11, 1939.

[3] See Ronald E. Powaski, *The Cold War: The United States and the Soviet Union, 1917–1991* (Oxford and New York: Oxford University Press, 1998); Serei N. Goncharov, John W. Lewis, and Xue Litai, *Uncertain Partners: Stalin, Mao, and the Korean War* (Stanford, CA: Stanford University Press, 1993) and Leland M. Goodrich, *Korea: A Study of U.S. Policy in the United Nations* (New York: Council on Foreign Relations, 1956).

[4] Deirdre Griswold, "Why Bush Should Study History," *Pyongyang, Democratic People's Republic of Korea*, Reprinted from the 9 May 2002 issue of *Workers World Newspaper*. See also Harold F. Cook, "Early American Contacts with Korea," *Transactions of the Royal Asiatic Society, Korea Branch* 55 (1980): 87.

[5] See Leonid A. Petrov, "The Rise of the Socio-economic School and the Formation of North Korean Official Historiography," Unpublished Ph.D. Thesis, Canberra: The Australian National University, 2002, p. 283. Kim Il Sung also described his great grandfather's role in the *General Sherman* incident in his autobiography, *With The Century*. Kim Il Sung, *With The Century*, vol.1 (P'yŏngyang: Foreign Languages Publishing House, 1992).

[6] See Kongdan Oh and Ralph C. Hassig, *North Korea: Through the Looking Glass* (Washington, D.C.: Brookings Institution Press, 2000), p. 100.

[7] See Leonid Petrov, "Restoring the Glorious Past: North Korean Juch'e Historiography and Koguryô," (Paper presented at Academy of Korean Studies, Seoul, Korea. March 25, 2004).

[8] Chan Sup Chang and Nahn Joo Chang, *The Korean Management System: Cultural, Political, Economic Foundations* (Westport, CT: Quorum Books, 1994), p. 35.

[9] Lee, *A New History of Korea*, p. 324–325.

Glossary of Korean Terms

Korean terms are romanized using the McCune-Reischauer method. There are some exceptions, for example, in cases where the common usage for terms such as *Namdaemun* or *dae kiôp* will be used.

Anchông 안정   (stability, security) Confucian ethic of stability.

Bukdaemun 북대문   (Great North Gate) One of the four major entrances to the walled city of Seoul. As with much of the city's fortifications, in the wake of urban growth it was gradually dismantled.

chang in 장인   (artisans) For much of the Early Chosôn Dynasty, the Korean government excised control over craftsmen and artisans. Goods, like weaponry, textiles, paper, furniture, and pottery were manufactured for local governments, court officials, or the elites. By the Late Chosôn Period, new laws and the formation of craft guilds stimulated widespread commercial production of goods, most often for distribution by the merchant class.

chabonjuûi maengaron 자본주의 맹알온   (capitalist sprouts) Korean nationalist theory that indigenous development of capitalism "sprouted" in the Late Chosôn Period.

Chosôn 조선   Korean dynasty founded in 1392 by Yi Song Kye (King T'aejo). The name dates back to the establishment of first legendary Korean state, *Chosôn*, soon after the mythical founding of the Korean people by *Tan'gun* in 2333 BC.

chumak 주막   (vine tents) Located near Korea's open-air markets, these small taverns served food and drink most often to traders and merchants. In some instances, they also served as venues for prostitution.

chungin 중인   (middle people) Hereditary caste of clerks, doctors, astronomers, architects, geomancers, interpreters, scribes, and technicians who served the *yangban* and the monarchy. Their early interactions with the West led to many of them becoming agents of reform and modernization, while others capitalized on their skills to accumulate wealth and means.

ch'ôkhwapi 척화비   (stone pillars) Stone monument erected across Korea to proclaim royal edicts and acknowledge historic events.

ch'ônmin 천민   (despised people) Hereditary class of Koreans in the lowest level of social stratification. They included a number of groups such as *kisaeng* (concubines), slaves, entertainers, *paekchông* (butchers and meat-handlers). In *Chosôn* society, some of these groups lived outside society as untouchables.

ch'ône 천에   (hooded garb) In Chosôn society, norms dictated that *yangban* women were publicly required to wear hooded garb called *ch'ône* outside the confines of the sanctuary of the homes.

dae kiôp 대기업 (large-scale business) Modern term for South Korean conglomerates such as LG, Samsung, Hyundai, and SK. Characteristics of these conglomerates include their family-management model and often unrelated diversification of their businesses. Following the Asian fiscal crisis of 1997, government, public, and international banking institutions have mandated restructuring among the large business groups. This mandate has led to the firms to focus their operations on three-to-four core business sectors, foster stockholder transparency, shift from a market share emphasis to a profit driven business model, reduce family control, and permit foreign stockownership.

Hansông chôn'gi hoesa 한성 전기 회사   (Seoul Electric Company) Established in 1897 under King Kojong's edict for modernization. Koreans Yi Kûnbae and Kim Tusûng initially headed the company with Henry Collbran and Harry Bostwick overseeing its construction and operation.

hwajôn 전   (fire arrow) Traditional projectile weapon of Korean military, some of which could rocket eight hundred feet and then explode. With the increased introduction of western armaments in the nineteenth century, the projectiles were like many of the Korean military arms outdated.

hwaldong sajin 활동 사진   (motion picture) Introduced in 1903 to the Korean public by Henry Collbran's firm, its interest grew so that by 1905 films shown at the Tongdaemun *hwaldong sajin* located near the Tongdaemun (Great East Gate) were quite popular among urban Koreans.

inhwa 인화   (harmony) Confucian value that fosters harmony in society and among co-workers.

Kabo Kyôngjang 갑오경장   1894 far-reaching progressive Korean domestic reforms numbering between 600-to-1,000. Some scholars suggest the reforms came under pressure from Japanese authorities, while others feel they were part of Korea's self-strengthening drive towards modernization.

kaekchu 객주   (commission agents) With the rise of Korean commerce in the late Chosôn Period, a group of intermediates between the merchants in rural regions and traders in Korea's cities developed. These agents accumulated capital that led to additional ventures such as money lending and warehousing of goods.

kaehang 개항   (opening of ports) Term that describes the Korea's opening to foreign interactions in Early Modern Era.

kimch'i 김 치   Perhaps Korea's most famous indigenous food made with Chinese cabbage that is fermented with red pepper, fish paste, and spices. Actually there are seasonal and regional varieties of the food made from many vegetables including radishes and cucumbers.

Kojong Sillok 고종 실록   Specific historic record of Korea's twenty-sixth monarch, King Kojong (1863–1907). The *sillok* were chronologies begun after the reign of the Chosôn Dynasty's first king, T'aejo, by court historians. With each successive ruler they covered politics, foreign relations, economy, military, law, communications and transportation and religion of the Chosôn Dynasty

kôbuksôn 거북선 (turtle boat) Warship created by Korean Admiral Yi Sun-Shin in 1591 who foresaw an imminent invasion by the Japanese. Seen as unrivaled in the period, the ruggedly constructed covered ship was ironclad and navigated by oars and sail. A dragonhead on its bow and turtle tail on its stern added to the ship's formidable appearance.

kukôn che 1 ho 구건 제 1 호   (Warship Number 1) The re-named *General Sherman*.

Namdaemun 남대문   (Great South Gate) One of the four major entrances to the walled city of Seoul. As one of the few remaining gates, the Korean cultural presentation program has assigned the structure as National Cultural Asset #1. The gate is also called *Sungnyemun*—Gate of Noble Ceremony.

makkôlli 막걸리 (rice wine) Popular Korean alcoholic drink made from fermented rice.

Miguk 미국   (beautiful nation) Korean name for the United States of America.

paekchông 백정 Members of the *ch'ônmin*, they served as butchers, leatherworkers, gravediggers, and executioners in Chosôn society. Perhaps, the most segregated of Korea's (and Japan's) lowest caste, prejudice against the group continued into the twentieth century.

poram 보람   (worthiness) Confucian virtue that values satisfaction in one's work.

Posin'gak (Boshingak) 보신각   Once called the *Chonggak* (literally bell pavilion) the building's name was changed to Boshingak (universal trust pavilion) in 1895 during the reign of King Kojong. The pavilion dates back to the founding of the Chosôn Dynasty in the late fourteenth century.

sadaebu 사대부   (scholarly officials) Ruling bureaucrats of Korea's *yangban* class, who oversaw key governmental positions. Hereditary officeholders their administrative positions became increasingly influenced by factionalism, regionalism, and cronyism.

sangin 상인   (merchants) For eons Korean traders oversaw commerce most often with neighboring China and Japan. The merchants of Seoul, Pusan, Kaesông, and in market areas near the mouth of the Yalu River and on towns on the Korean-Manchurian border catered to both the needs of the *yangban* elite and privateers. Goods traded included Korean ginseng, Japanese copper, and Chinese silver. Domestically, merchants benefited from economic change in the Early Modern Era and accumulated wealth—often in cash rather than land. In turn these merchants, as financiers, funded production of goods by artisans and craftsmen—goods the merchants distributed and sold for profit. With the opening of Korea to the West, successful merchants were well positioned to benefit from expanding western style market system, new commercial opportunity, and industry.

sangmin 상민 (common people) Freeborn peasants who served a tenant or landed farmers. They ranked below *yangban* and the *chungin* in Korean social stratification. Interestingly in Neo-Confucian society farmers ranked above artisans and merchants since they were highly regarded as producers.

Sôdaemun 서대문 (Great West Gate) One of the four major entrances to the walled city of Seoul.

Sinmi yangyo 신미양요 (The American disturbance of 1871) Term given to American military action that saw U.S. troops engaging Korean soldiers on Kanghwa Island. The American motive for the entering Korean waters was to secure a treaty, however with little success and escalating confrontations, they withdrew. Subsequently, the Korean regent proclaimed that success in repelling the foreigners was a confirmation of his strict isolationist-nativist policy.

sirhak 실학 (practical learning) Late Chosôn Dynasty intellectual movement that looked to new sources of information from China and the West. On one level it manifested in re-examination of traditional values, while exploring new skills in agriculture, education, technology, medicine, and commerce.

Sungnyemun 숭례문 (Gate of Noble Ceremony) *See Namdaemun*

Tongdaemun 동대문 (Great East Gate) One of the four major entrances to the walled city of Seoul. With the Namdaemun, the Great East Gate still remains as a cultural and historic landmark. The gate is also called the *Hwanginchimun*—Gate in Delight in Goodness.

Tongnip Sinmun 동닙 신문   (*The Independent News*) Korean language newspaper established in 1896 by progressive, reform-minded nationalist that included noted reformer Sô Chaep'il. The paper was published in *hangul* (the indigenous Korean written script) and had an English language section.

t'angp'yôngch'aek 탕평 책   (policy of impartiality) Korea's nineteenth century state policy of isolationism, which became a trademark of the Taewon'gun administration.

T'ongnikimuamun 통리기무아문   (Office of General Management) Formed in 1881, it was a move to modernize Korea through self-strengthening. Its mandates were far-reaching and restructured Korea's military, foreign matters, industry, trade, and education.

yangban 양반   (two classes) At the apex of Korean Neo-Confucian social stratification, this hereditary elitist caste dominated the Chosôn Dynasty through land ownership and office holding. Seen as literati-scholars their position in Confucian society meant they devoted considerable time in study of Chinese Confucian classics or the fine arts.

yôgak 여각   (brokers; traveler counselors) Like their peers, the *kaekchu,* these entrepreneurs accumulated capital through trade and movement of goods across Korea. By the early Modern Era a few successful brokers entered industry and banking, along with investment in land.

Bibliography

Primary and Secondary Sources

Allen, Horace N. *Things Korean: A Collection of Sketches and Anecdotes Missionary and Diplomatic.* New York: Fleming H. Revell Company, 1908.

Arnold, Dean Alexander. *American Economic Enterprises in Korea, 1895–1939.* New York: Arno Press, 1976.

_____. "Collbran of Colorado: Concessionaire in Korea." *Colorado Quarterly* (Summer 1959).

Baker, Don. "A Different Thread: Orthodoxy, Heterodoxy, and Catholicism in a Confucian World." *Culture and the State in Late Chosôn Korea.* Edited by Ja Hyun Kim Haboush and Martina Deuchler. Cambridge, MA: Harvard University Press, 1999.

Buss, Claude A. "At the Beginning." *Reflections on a Century of United States-Korean Relations, Conference Papers, June 1982.* Washington, D.C.: Academy of Korean Studies and The Wilson Center, University Press of America, 1983.

Cable, E.M. "United States-Korean Relations, 1866–1871." *Transactions of the Korea Branch of the Royal Asiatic Society* 28 (1938).

Chang, Chan Sup and Nahn Joo Chang. *The Korean Management System: Cultural, Political, Economic Foundations.* Westport, CT: Quorum Books, 1994.

Chang, Gordon H. "Whose 'Barbarism'? Whose 'Treachery'? Race and Civilization in the Unknown United States-Korea War of 1871." *The Journal of American History* 89 (2003).

Chien, Fredrick Foo. *The Opening of Korea: A Study of Chinese Diplomacy, 1876–1885.* Hamden, CT: The Shoe String Press, Inc., 1967.

Choe, Ching Young. *The Rule of the Tae Won' Gun, 1864–1873: Restoration in Yi Korea.* Cambridge, MA: Harvard East Asian Monographs, 1972.

Chung, Chai-Sik. A *Korean Encounter with the Western World*. Berkeley, CA: Institute of East Asian Studies, University of California at Berkeley, 1995.

Chung, Kae H. "An Overview of Korean Management." *Korean Managerial Dynamics*. Edited by Kae H. Chung and Hak Chong Lee. New York: Praeger, 1989.

Clark, Donald, N. *Living Dangerously in Korea: The Western Experience 1900–1950*. Norwalk, CT: EastBridge Press, 2003.

Conroy, Hilary. *The Japanese Seizure of Korea: 1868–1910, The Study of Realism and Idealism in International Relations*. Philadelphia, PA: University of Pennsylvania Press, 1960.

Cook, Harold F. "Early American Contacts with Korea." *Transactions of the Royal Asiatic Society, Korea Branch* 55 (1980).

_____. *Pioneer American Businessman in Korea: The Life and Times of Walter Davis Townsend*. Seoul: Royal Asiatic Society, Korea Branch, 1981.

Crapol, Edward P. *James G. Blaine: Architect of Empire*. Wilmington, DE: SR Books, 2000.

Cumings, Bruce. *Korea's Place in the Sun: A Modern History*. New York: W.W. Norton, 1997.

Dennett, Tyler. *Americans in Eastern Asia: A Critical Study of United States' Policy in the Far East in the Nineteenth Century*. 1922, New York: Barnes & Noble, 1963.

Deuchler, Martina. *Confucian Gentlemen and Barbarian Envoys: The Opening of Korea, 1875–1885*. Seattle, WA: University of Washington, 1977.

_____. *The Confucian Transformation of Korea*. Cambridge, MA: Harvard University Press, 1992.

_____. "Tradition and Ideology: Korea's Initial Response to Christianity from a Religious and Sociological Perspective." *Asian Culture* 4 (October 1988).

Drake, Frederick C. *The Empire of the Seas: A Biography of Rear Admiral Robert Wilson Shufeldt, USN*. Honolulu, HI: University of Hawaii Press, 1984.

Drucker, Peter. *Innovation and Entrepreneurship: Practice and Principles*. New York: Harper and Row, 1985.

Duus, Peter. *The Abacus and the Sword: The Japanese Penetration of Korea, 1895–1910*. Berkeley, CA: University of California Press, 1995.

Eckert, Carter J. *Offspring of Empire: The Koch'ang Kims and the Colonial Origins of Korean Capitalism, 1876–1945*. Seattle, WA: University of Washington, 1991.

Gale, James Scarth. "The Fate of the General Sherman." *The Korean Repository*. Vol. 2. New York: Paragon Book Reprint Corp., 1964.

"General Sherman chôn" (제너럴셰만호젼). *Han'guk Minjok Munhwa Taebaekkwa Sajon*. Kyonggi-do Songnam-si.

Griffis, William Elliot. *Corea, The Hermit Kingdom*. 1882; reprint, New York: Charles Scriber's Sons, 1897.

_____. *Corea: Without and Within*. Philadelphia, PA, 1885.

Goodrich, Leland M. *Korea: A Study of U.S. Policy in the United Nations*. New York: Council on Foreign Relations, 1956.

Goncharov, Serei N., John W. Lewis, and Xue Litai. *Uncertain Partners: Stalin, Mao, and the Korean War*. Stanford, CA: Stanford University Press, 1993.

Hamilton, Angus. *Korea*. London: W. Heinemann, 1904.

Harrington, Fred Harvey. "An American View of Korean-American Relations." *Korean-American Relations, 1866–1997*. Edited by Yur-Bok Lee and Wayne Patterson. Albany, NY: State University of New York Press, 1999.

_____. *God, Mammon, and the Japanese: Dr. Horace Allen and Korean-American Relations, 1884–1905*. Madison, WI: University of Wisconsin Press, 1944.

Henderson, Gregory. *The Politics of the Vortex*. Cambridge, MA: Harvard University Press, 1968.

Heyl, Erik. *Early American Steamers*. Vol. 1. Buffalo, New York, 1953.

Hulbert, Homer B. *Hulbert's The History of Korea*. Vol. 2. Edited by Clarence Norwood Weems. New York: Hillary House Publishers Ltd., 1962.

Hwang, Kyung Moon. *Beyond Birth: Social Status in the Emergence of Modern Korea* Cambridge, MA: Harvard University Press, 2004.

_____."From Dirt to Heaven: Northern Koreans in the Chosôn and Early Modern Eras," *Harvard Journal of Asiatic Studies*, 62 (June 2002).

Kim, Key-Hiuk. *The Last Phase of the East Asian World Order: Korea, Japan, and the Chinese Empire, 1860–1882*. Berkeley, CA: University of California Press, 1980.

Kim, Il Sung. *With The Century*. Vol.1. P'yŏngyang: Foreign Languages Publishing House, 1992.

Lee, Sun-keum. "Some Lesser-Known Facts About Taewongun and His Foreign Policy." *Transactions of the Korean Branch of the Royal Asiatic Society* 39 (1962).

Lee, Ki-Baek. *A New History of Korea*. Translated by Edward W. Wagner with Edward J. Shultz. Seoul, Korea: Ilchokak Publishers, 1984.

Lee, Peter, ed. *The Sourcebook of Korean Civilization*. Vol. 2. New York: Columbia, 1996.

Leeke, Ada E. and Evelyn Shaw. *When American Came to Korea*. Freeman, SD: Pine Hill Press, 1991.

Leibenstein, Harvey. T*he Collected Essays of Harvey Leibenstein*. Vol. 2. Edited by Kenneth Button. Aldershot, England: Edward Elgar Publishing, 1989.

Lincoln, Ashbrook. "San Francisco Bay-Area Views of Russian Aggression in Far East, 1903–1905." *California Historical Society Quarterly* 30 (1951).

Lone, Stewart and Gavan McCormick. *Korea: Since 1850*. New York: St. Martin Press, 1993.

Longford, Joseph H. *The Story of Korea*. London: T. Fisher Unwin, 1911.

Lytle, William M. and Forrest R. Holdcamper. *Merchant Steam Vessels of the U.S.: 1790–1868*. Edited by C. Bradford Mitchell. Staten Island, NY: The Steamship Historical Society of America, 1975.

Mills, Edwin W. "Gold Mining in Korea." *The Korean Branch of the Royal Asiatic Society* 7 (1916).

Marshall, Alfred. *Principles of Economics* 9th ed. New York: Macmillan, 1961.

McKenzie, F. A. *Korea's Fight for Freedom*. New York: Fleming H. Revell Company, 1920.

McNamara, Dennis L. *The Colonial Origins of Korean Enterprise, 1910–1945*. New York: Cambridge University Press, 1990.

Mundy, D.L. *God and Rich Society: A Study of Christians in a World of Abundance.* New York: Oxford University Press, 1961.

Myers, Robert J. *Korea in the Cross Currents: A Century of Struggle and the Crisis of Reunification.* New York: Palgrave, 2001.

Nahm, Andrew, ed. "American-Korean Relations, 1866–1878, An Overview." *The United States and Korea: American-Korean Relations, 1866–1976.* Kalamazoo, MI: The Center for Korean Studies, 1979.

Nelson, Melvin Frederick. *Korea and the Old Orders in Eastern Asia.* Baton Rouge, LA: Louisiana State University Press, 1945.

Oh, Kongdan and Ralph C. Hassig. *North Korea: Through the Looking Glass.* Washington, D.C.: Brookings Institution Press, 2000.

Oliver, Robert T. *A History of the Korean People in Modern Times: 1800 to Present.* London and Toronto: Associated University Presses, 1993.

Palais, James B. *Politics and the Policy in Traditional Korea.* Cambridge, MA: Harvard University Press, 1975.

Palmer, Spencer J. "American Gold Mining in Korea's Unsan District." *Pacific Historical Review* 31 (1962).

_____. Korea and Christianity: The Problem of Identification with Tradition. Seoul: Hollym, Royal Asiatic Society Branch, 1967.

Paolino, Ernest N. *The Foundations of The American Empire: William Henry Seward and The U.S. Foreign Policy.* Ithaca, NY: Cornell University Press, 1973.

Park Chan-Seung. "Should Korean Historians Abandon Nationalism?" *Korea Journal* (Summer 1999).

Park, Kyeyong. *The Korean American Dream: Immigrants and Small Business in New York City.* Ithaca, NY: Cornell University Press, 1997.

Paullin, Charles Oscar. *Diplomatic Negotiations of American Naval Officers, 1778–1883.* Baltimore, MD: Johns Hopkins Press, 1912.

Poggi, Gianfranco. *Calvinism and the Capitalist Spirit: Max Weber's Protestant Ethic.* Amherst, MA: University Of Massachusetts Press, 1983.

Powaski, Ronald E. *The Cold War: The United States and the Soviet Union, 1917–1991.* Oxford and New York: Oxford University Press, 1998.

Pratt, Keith and Richard Rutt. *Korea: A Historical and Cultural Dictionary.* Surrey, England: Curzon Press, 1999.

Pratt, Keith. *Old Seoul.* New York: Oxford University Press, 2002.

Rhee, M.J. *The Doomed Empire: Japan in Colonial Korea.* Brookfield, VT: Ashgate Publishing Company, 1997.

Ross, John. *History of Korea.* London: Elliot Stock, 1891.

Rutt, Richard. *James Scarth Gale and History of the Korean People.* Seoul: Korean Branch of the Royal Asiatic Society, 1972.

Ryu, Dae Young. "Understanding Early American Missionaries In Korea (1884–1910); Capitalist Middle-Class Values and the Weber Thesis." *Archives de Sciences Sociales des Religions* 113 (Javier-Mars 2001).

Sands, William Franklin. *Undiplomatic Memories: The Far East 1896–1904.* New York: Whittlesey House, 1930.

Simon, John Y., ed. *The Papers of Ulysses S. Grant.* Vol. 22. June 1, 1871–January 31, 1872. Carbondale, IL: Southern Illinois University Press, 1998.

Speer, William. "Corea: What Shall We Do," *The Galaxy.* Sheldon and Company, New York, 1872.

Stevenson, Howard H., Michael J. Roberts, et al. *New Business Ventures and the Entrepreneur.* Boston, MA: Irwin McGraw-Hill, 1999.

Swartout, Robert R., Jr. *Mandarins, Gunboats, and Power Politics: Owen Nickerson Denny and the International Rivalries in Korea.* Honolulu, HI: University Press of Hawaii, 1980.

Swisher, Earl. "The Adventures of Four Americans in Korea and Peking in 1855." *Pacific Historical Review* 21 (August 1952).

_____. *China's Management of the American Barbarians: A Study of Sino-American Relations, 1841–1861, with Documents.* New York: Octagon Books, 1972.

Underwood, Horace G. *The Call of Korea: Political-Social-Religious.* New York: Fleming H. Revell Company, 1908.

Underwood, Lilias Horton. *Fifteen Years Among the Top-Knots.* Seoul: Royal Asiatic Society, Korea Branch, Kyung-In Publishing Co., 1977.

Wagner, Edward, Carter Eckert, et al. *Korea: Old and New, A History*. Cambridge, MA: Harvard University Press, 1990.

Wauzzinski, Robert. *Between God and Gold: Protestant Evangelicalism and the Industrial Revolution, 1820–1914*. Rutherford, NJ: Fairleigh Dickenson University Press, 1993.

Weber, Max. *The Protestant Ethic and the Spirit of Capitalism*. Translated by Talcott Parsons. New York: Routledge, 2002.

Whan, Oh Moon "The Two Visits of the Reverend R. J. Thomas to Korea." *Transactions of the Korean Branch of the Royal Asiatic Society* 22 (1933).

Yi, Kyu-tae. *Modern Transformation of Korea*. Translated by Sung Tong-mahn, Charles Goldberg, et al. Seoul: Sejong Publishing Company, 1970.

Government Publications and Documents

Washington, U.S. Government. Printing Office. *Papers Relating to the Foreign Relations of the United States, 1861–1928*, 1867, 1868, and 1871.

H. Doc. Extension of American Commerce-Proposed Mission to Japan and Corea, 28th Cong. 2nd Sess. 15 February 1845. U.S. Congress, Executive Documents. Vol. 3.

File Microcopies of Records in the National Archives. no. 112, roll 3, National Archives, Washington, D.C.

Periodicals

"Choson Gold." *Time Magazine* (September 11, 1939).

Gendron, George. "Flashes of Genius." *Inc. Magazine* (May 1996).

Griswold, Deirdre. "Why Bush Should Study History." *Pyongyang, Democratic People's Republic of Korea*. Reprinted *Workers World Newspaper* (May 9, 2002).

Newspapers

Chosun Ilbo (October 30, 2002).

Tongnip Sinmun (*The Independent*) (May 1897 and September 1899).

Collections

Allen Manuscripts. New York Public Library, New York, NY.

Henry Collbran Papers. Colorado State Historical Society, Denver, CO.

Kojong Sunjong Sillok. Han'guk Kyohoe yôn'guso. Seoul: T'amguadang, 1970.

Unpublished Papers and Dissertations

Petrov, Leonid A. "Restoring the Glorious Past: North Korean Juch'e Historiography and Koguryô." Academy of Korean Studies. Seoul, Korea. March 25, 2004.

_____. "The Rise of the Socio-economic School and the Formation of North Korean Official Historiography." Unpublished PhD Thesis, Canberra: The Australian National University, 2002.

Photograph, Illustration, and Map Credits

I am grateful for the collections, archives, and publications that have contributed photographs, illustrations, and maps to this work. Moreover, every effort has been made to acknowledge the photographs, illustrations, and maps' sources.

Front piece 1: Chosôn Map: Courtesy of Trustees, British Library. London, England.

Front piece 2: Western Map of Korea. Courtesy of the author.

Fig. 1.1 Courtesy of the LG Group. Seoul, South Korea.

Fig. 1.2 Courtesy of Hyundai Motor America. Fountain Valley, CA.

Fig. 1.3 Courtesy of Hyundai Motor America. Fountain Valley, CA; Kia Motors America. Irvine, CA; Samsung Electronics. Seoul, Korea; and LG Electronics. Seoul, Korea.

Fig. 2.1 Namdaemun painting. Source unknown.

Fig. 2.2 Courtesy of The National Museum of Korea. Seoul, South Korea.

Fig. 2.3 Courtesy of The National Museum of Korea. Seoul, South Korea.

Fig. 2.4 Courtesy of Yi Dong Ju Private Collection, Seoul, South Korea.

Fig. 2.5 Courtesy of Samuel Moffett Collection, Princeton Theological Seminar Libraries.

Fig. 2.6 Courtesy of Project Gutenberg's *Corea or Cho-sen*, by A (Arnold) Henry Savage-Landor.

Fig. 2.7 Courtesy of Samuel Moffett Collection, Princeton Theological Seminar Libraries.

Fig. 2.8 Source: *Choson sidai* (*The Chosen Period*), vol. 1.

Fig. 2.9 Courtesy of City of Pusan. Pusan Metropolitan City Museum. Pusan Local Cultural Asset #18. Pusan, South Korea.

Fig. 2.10 Photograph of Taewon'gun. Source unknown.

Map 2.1 Courtesy of the author.

Fig. 3.1 Courtesy of U.S. Naval Historical Center. Artwork by Erik Heyl.

Map 3.1 Courtesy of the author.

Fig. 3.2 Courtesy of Samuel Moffett Collection, Princeton Theological Seminar Libraries.

Fig. 4.1 Courtesy of *Transactions of the Korean Branch of the Royal Asiatic Society* 22 (1933), Oh Moon Whan," The Two Visits of the Reverend R. J. Thomas to Korea."

Fig. 4.2 Courtesy of U.S. Navy Observatory Library Archives, Washington, D.C.

Fig. 4.3 Photograph credited to Felice Beato.

Fig. 5.1 Courtesy of Project Gutenberg's *Corea or Cho-sen*, by A (Arnold) Henry Savage-Landor.

Fig. 5.2 Courtesy of National Anthropological Archives, Smithsonian Institution, Washington, D.C. Photo credited to H. Higuchi.

Fig. 6.1 Courtesy of *Choson Ilbo*. Seoul, South Korea.

Fig. 6.2 Courtesy of Presbyterian Historical Society. Philadelphia, PA.

Fig. 6.3 Courtesy of Courtesy of *Korea*, Angus Hamilton.

Map 6.1 Sketch map Sôul, from a paper by C.T. Gardner, 1895. Source unknown.

Map 6.2 Courtesy of Trustees, British Library. London, England.

Fig. 6.4 Courtesy of Samuel Moffett Collection, Princeton Theological Seminar Libraries.

Fig. 6.5 Courtesy of *Korea*, Angus Hamilton.

Fig. 6.6 Courtesy of *Fifteen Years Among the Top-knots or Life in Korea*, L.H. Underwood.

Fig. 6.7–6.8 Courtesy of Samuel Moffett Collection, Princeton Theological Seminar Libraries.

Fig. 6.9 Courtesy of the Colorado Historical Society. Denver, CO.

Fig. 6.10 Courtesy of *Book on Views of Korea*, (title in Japanese with no publisher and date).

Fig. 6.11–6.13 Courtesy of Samuel Moffett Collection, Princeton Theological Seminar Libraries.

Fig. 6.14 Courtesy of *Things Korean: A Collection of Sketches and Anecdotes Missionary and Diplomatic,* Horace Allen.

Fig. 6.15 Courtesy of Western History Collection. Denver Public Library, Denver, CO.

Fig. 7.1 Courtesy of Samuel Moffett Collection, Princeton Theological Seminar Libraries.

Fig. 7.2 Courtesy of Dr. Robert Sayers.

Fig. 7.3 Courtesy of *Transactions of the Korean Branch of the Royal Asiatic Society* 7 (1916), Edwin W. Mills, "Gold Mining in Korea."

Fig. 7.4–7.7 Courtesy of Samuel Moffett Collection, Princeton Theological Seminar Libraries.

Fig. 7.8 Courtesy of Horace H. Underwood.

Fig. 7.9 Underwood Typewriter advertisement. Source unknown.

Fig. 7.10 Courtesy of *Choson sindai* (*The Chosen Period*), vol. 1.

Fig. 8.1 Courtesy of *Book on Views of Korea*, (title in Japanese with no publisher and date).

Fig. 8.2 Courtesy of *Korean Web Weekly.*

Fig. 8.3 Courtesy of *Choson Ilbo.* Seoul, South Korea.

Index

978-0-595-37068-9
0-595-37068-3